"EASY TO READ AND INFUS⸺ ⸺ Fatio's book encourages older people to combat negative stereotypes about aging and to live a full and exciting life. With its inspirational anecdotes and practical advice, this book will convince you that "to celebrate life is to celebrate aging."

SUSANNE PAUL, PRESIDENT, GLOBAL ACTION ON AGING

"AgeEsteem hits at a crucial time when baby boomers begin to retire. Getting older does not always come with celebration. Bonnie Fatio challenges us to change our thinking about aging and teaches us how. Bonnie practices what she writes. She models leadership and her book will break barriers of age for anyone who reads AgeEsteem."

DR. MUSIMBI KANYORO , GENERAL SECRETARY, WORLDYWCA

"Bonnie Fatio reveals how she "lives the zest" in this beautiful, insightful, much needed book, AgeEsteem. Ageless and timeless. The internationally respected expert, speaker and trainer in motivation, Bonnie lights the path to transformation. In my early 40s I can testify that AgeEsteem is a must-read for anyone at any age, the earlier the better."

AMY BALDERSON, FOUNDER OF LEGACY

Bonnie Lou Fatio has an infectious personality, bounds with enthusiasm and ignites energy wherever she goes. AgeEsteem ingeniously reflects her. You will find cleverly carved out dignified, fun aging possibilities in this ground breaking magnificent gift to humanity.

DR. JUDITH GERHART
FOUNDER OF WOMEN OF WEALTH AND WELLNESS

Bonnie Lou Fatio
author and founder of AgeEsteem·

AgeEsteem.®

GROWING A *POSITIVE* ATTITUDE TOWARD AGING

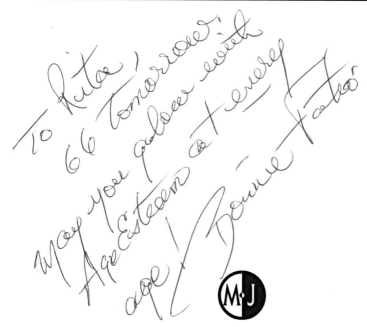

MORGAN JAMES PUBLISHING • NEW YORK

AgeEsteem®

GROWING A *POSITIVE* ATTITUDE TOWARD AGING

ISBN: 978-1-60037-268-1 (Hardcover)
ISBN: 978-1-60037-267-4 (Paperback)

Published by:

MORGAN · JAMES™
THE ENTREPRENEURIAL PUBLISHER
www.morganjamespublishing.com

Morgan James Publishing, LLC
1225 Franklin Ave Ste 32
Garden City, NY 11530-1693
Toll Free 800-485-4943
www.MorganJamesPublishing.com

Cover/Interior Design by:
Rachel Campbell
rachel@r2cdesign.com

Cover Photograph:
James Drew

Biography Photograph:
David Muenker

Habitat
for Humanity®
Peninsula
Building Partner

WHAT OTHERS ARE SAYING

"**SOME PEOPLE HAVE THE ENERGY** and desire to change the world - Bonnie has that energy and desire to make us all look at aging differently, positively. What she writes in *AgeEsteem* makes you want to be part of this change. The stories are delightful, the ideas thought provoking – a great new way to look at the world of getting older."

JOYCE FEINBERG, TEXAS

"If you want a positive, delightful way to think about aging, Bonnie Fatio inspires it. Reading this book can spark you and those around you to age with pizzaz!"

BRIAN JACOBSON, CANADA

"Bonnie is one of those natural storytellers whose passion for making the world better thru AgeEsteem is inspiring. How much better we would all be if we lived these pages."

HENRY STROBER, MICHIGAN

"I am so very proud to be an AgeEsteemer! Your writing is superb! It was like you were talking directly to me. I loved the "autobiographical" content. I felt very close to you. People can get so much motivation from this book."

EVIE BREAKSTONE, CALIFORNIA

"Your examples are delightful, esp. the Deb light bulb moment. And, of course, the little boy's question: "Are you dead, lady?""

Suzanne Hough, Oklahoma

"From poignant to rib-tickling, these insightful stories and techniques inspire me to live my life fully at every age."

Rose Muenker, Colorado

"Bonnie has a very special gift of being able to communicate to people from the heart."

Beth Houseman, New York

"Bonnie's "live in the moment" and the "letting go" segments have really ministered to me. Why oh why is it so hard to let go sometimes?"

Debby Phelps, Louisiana

"AgeEsteem is an awareness of the value of my whole life: young – mid-life and older."

Denis Grote, Colorado

"I am in a dramatic/traumatic life phase – and am freeing myself. These specific tips and thoughts for positive thinking of AgeEsteem are my new foundation."

Suzanna Rudolph, Michigan

"AgeEsteem has application for everyone from young to old."

Elvira Fairfield, Florida

"This is a real inspiration, not only very well done but because of the fact that Bonnie is really trying to change the world."

Gladys Foster, Colorado

"AgeEsteem is a thought provoking experience – which moves us towards a new way to think of aging that is positive."

PETER BAKER, UNITED KINGDOM

"AgeEsteem teaches you how to appreciate the age you are with real self esteem. I will live more confidently with myself, appreciating the well-aged value I bring to my own life experience and the lives of others."

DAVID R. REED, COLORADO

"AgeEsteem is a wonderful guide to reflect about life, experiences, lessons, and above all, the opportunity to think about and share "my legacy of lessons" and to go for "outrageous acts". For those "still working" like me, it helps to re-establish a better balance between Professional, Personal and Private life matters."

ROBERT HUCK, SWITZERLAND

"You bring immense talent, expertise and energy! You are an amazing woman, Bonnie, proud of your age and willing to put it to good use. I am looking forward to gaining more AgeEsteem."

DAISY ROSE, GHANA

"AgeEsteem is a very interesting approach to addressing the aging process not only of the body, but to the mind where that state can be altered/challenged to view the process as an adventure."

RICH PHELPS, LOUISIANNA

"3 weeks after the w.i.n. conference I am still very exited about "AgeEsteem". I already caught the AgeEsteem bug. It was a very interesting and rewarding day with you."

BÉATRICE MEIER, AUSTRALIA

"AgeEsteem is a fabulous idea. I am happy that Bonnie has the ability and daring to create this vision." ALEXANDRA WOOG, SWITZERLAND

"AgeEsteem is very inspiring and fun. Every time I get a boost of energy. You are such an inspiring person Bonnie."

MICHÈLE LONGPRÉ, FRANCE

"Thank you Bonnie for this new perspective on age. It works!"

VIRGINIA BOND, MISSISSIPPI

ACKNOWLEDGEMENTS

MANY WONDERFUL PEOPLE SURROUND ME, encourage me and reach out to help me succeed. Mentors and friends from previous generations continue to inspire me. To these models and mentors I dedicate this first AgeEsteem® book with special recognition to my parents, Shirley Blewfield and James Russell Pollock.

My loving gratitude embraces my husband Gérard and our daughter Laetitia whose words, "You can do it." constantly overflow with love and practical encouragement.

My thanks extends to Judi Hall, my voice coach, who was involved before AgeEsteem had a name; Rose Muenker, my sister and professional confident; Amy Balderson Junod my precious star spinner; Delbert Jolley, my spiritual mentor for half a century; and Joyce Feinberg who is always there for me. James Drew, who conceived and photographed the cover photo; Helen Drew, my web wizard; David Muenker, personal photographer and friend; Musimbi Kanyoro who constantly inspires me; Diana Johnson, for her loving encouragement; Joan Baenziger for her hours of proofing; and the many people who have shown me wonderful aspects of aging.

In order to accomplish our dreams we need to believe in ourselves and to have that belief reinforced by others. This belief is what keeps us going when doubts begin to take over. Thank you to each of my doubt busters and supporters, many of whom are listed in the final pages of this book.

THE COVER PHOTO

The moment was fun, daring and delicious.

AS JAMES STARTED TO PUT his camera away, I pushed myself to a sitting position on the moist grass. We both burst into laughter.

What you don't see when you look at the cover of this book is the scene that surrounds me.

When James presented his idea for this cover with me lying in the grass, I immediately knew it was right. It was spunky and fun, yet natural. Anyone could do it or had done it at some point in life, so everyone could identify with it.

I pictured myself lying in the grass in our little yard. James had another idea.

He found the perfect spot in a small park which provides a short cut between two business districts. It's also where the Wall of the Reformation, one of the most frequented tourist sights in Geneva, is found.

Take another look at the cover and imagine the following scene.

People in business attire are racing to appointments. Parents pushing strollers, gardeners tending the flowers, groups of tourists and dogs pulling on leashes surround me. Oh, yes, James had chosen well! And in the midst of it all, just out of the reach of the sprinklers, there I am, lying on the grass revelling in the moment.

The moment was fun, daring and delicious. Who cares that a banker friend took me aside a few days later to discretely ask me, "Was that really you I saw lying in the park last week?"

AgeEsteem is LIVING moments that are fun, daring and delicious.

TABLE OF CONTENTS

INTRODUCTION

No matter where you are in your journey of life,
growing and aging continue to be companions.

WELCOME TO AGEESTEEM®: Growing a Positive Attitude Toward Aging. No matter where you are in your journey of life, growing and aging continue to be companions. As you gaze towards the horizon of future years and imagine how you want to live those years, having AgeEsteem will help you to view your own aging positively.

When I began the adventure of writing this book my thought was, "If I can grow my own AgeEsteem and feel good about aging, anyone can." I still believe this. If I am able to use these techniques, to grow AgeEsteem, so can you!

Age is a state of mind. We live our age from the inside out.

A perfect example of someone with AgeEsteem is Doris whose story follows in *A Model of AgeEsteem.* I love her example because it illustrates important keys to living with AgeEsteem.

- ❋ A positive attitude and gratitude are constant companions.
- ❋ We recognize that we have choices.
- ❋ We take responsibility for our happiness.
- ❋ How we speak to ourselves and the words we use influence our quality of life.
- ❋ We control our thoughts.
- ❋ We become what we see ourselves to be.
- ❋ Each of us needs a raison d'être, a purpose in life to guide us.
- ❋ Our special purpose doesn't need to change the universe, simply to improve our own little segment of the world.

All of these are addressed in the following pages.

As a motivational trainer and coach I have worked over the past 25 years with hundreds of clients who were living a contented life and enjoying a healthy self image until a-g-e suddenly became associated with o-l-d. From one moment to the next they saw themselves as less important and no longer significant.

I refer to this as an age attack.

For some it comes and goes in a flash, but it leaves a sensation of hollowness that is hard to cure. For others it settles in and keeps chipping away at their self-esteem.

A few months before my 60th birthday my husband casually asked me how I would like to celebrate. His question sent me into my one bout with age attack. (See *From Doubts to Dreams and Daring*.) It left me feeling alone in a desert of negative thoughts. It was a lonely place to be, but I didn't want to step forward into the future where I would become old.

Fortunately I have a very positive side that likes to dominate. She pushed her way into my thoughts saying, "So big deal. You're not the only one to turn 60. Don't dwell in the dark, step out here in the sunshine and decide what you're going to do about it!"

I actually knew what I wanted to do. For months I had felt that I was on the threshold of something. It was as though my whole life and career had been preparing me for something greater, but I just didn't know what it could be.

It was out of this black stupor that the idea of AgeEsteem® was born. Self-esteem needs to be reinforced in new ways as it becomes threatened by age. Self-esteem is not enough. We also need AgeEsteem. We need to feel good about ourselves at the age we are.

When you grow AgeEsteem, you make choices
based on your own needs and desires.

How many older people do you know who radiate interest and energy? How many younger people do you know who lack both these qualities? The former seem younger to us because we associate youth with curiosity and vitality. Age is a state of mind. We live our age from the inside out. AgeEsteem is critical to living with curiosity and vitality.

Daily we are bombarded by messages that become stamped into our subconscious, even though our intellectual, rational, knowledgeable consciousness does not buy into the image. We are confronted by advertisements that show beautiful, flawless skin on wrinkleless faces defining for our subconscious how we should look.

These messages are subtle – and not so subtle – and constant. They wear away at our self-image until we believe there is something wrong with us because we let our personality show. And yet, who would I be without my laugh lines? Why would I want to erase the proof on my brow that I am experienced at living?

I use this example about wrinkles here because it is one of many that express why we may feel less confident as we age.

AgeEsteem allows you to take and keep control of your life.

The goal of AgeEsteem is to help you feel good about yourself at the age you are today, every day. When you develop your AgeEsteem, you make knowledgeable choices based on your own needs and desires. AgeEsteem allows you to take and keep control of your life.

AgeEsteem®: Growing a Postive Attitude Toward Aging is written to help you develop your AgeEsteem. Journey through its pages. Stop from time to time to relate the message to your own life. Test the concept. Adapt it to your own needs. Adopt it as your own. Build it into your thoughts and life. Share it lavishly.

In my research for this book I have consulted many sources and studies as well as conducting personal interviews. Studies or research that I refer to are based on a number of different resources and are therefore to be considered general information.

The purpose of this book is to help you redevelop your thinking toward growing older, to facilitate your acceptance of your own aging and to enhance your image of age.

We do not stop the clock. We move forward with new energy and, yes, even enthusiasm. Age is not something to fear. If we do fear growing older, we are fighting against a natural phenomenon. Our fear induces us to place obstacles, self-imposed barriers, in our path. We limit ourselves and impede our joy of living, loving and contributing to the world. We need AgeEsteem to set ourselves free.

*Only you can make the age that you are living
and the years to follow what you want them to be.*

AgeEsteem®: Growing a Positive Attitude Towards Aging is written to inspire and to challenge. If the rest of your life is going to be fulfilling and happy, it is up to you. No one else can do it for you, not your reconstructive surgeon, not your doctor, not your family, not your spiritual coach. Only you can make the age that you are living and the years to follow what you want them to be.

I hope you will treat this book like a friend and mentor. Keep a notebook and pen nearby to note ideas and practice the exercises. Get acquainted

with its messages. Reach out and test its techniques and concepts. Rise to
its challenges.

Experiment and enjoy!

A MODEL OF AgeEsteem

You are the author of your own story.

DORIS IS A LIVING EXAMPLE of AgeEsteem. Doris lives in a retirement home in Arizona. She lost two husbands, both of whom had Alzheimer's during their last years. Following the death of her second husband, I asked Doris how she managed to remain so cheerful despite her grief.

She explained, "I keep a routine and get up to go down for breakfast each morning at 7am to get my motor lubricated. But before I even open my eyes in the morning, I listen for the birds and say thank you for the day. I remind myself that I can lie in bed and cultivate my aches and pains, or I can bounce out of bed and greet the day. It's more fun to greet the day!"

"And no matter how I feel when I wake up, the moment I leave my room I put a smile on my face. And do you know what happens? When I smile and think happy thoughts, even before I reach the elevator, I feel happy! My role in life is to be full of sunshine for others."

Choose to be happy.

If you emulate the example of Doris as you greet your day, make choices, choose a positive vocabulary and control your attitude to be congruent with your purpose, you will enjoy AgeEsteem.

The stories, quotes, tips, techniques and challenges that follow will help you to enrich your life with AgeEsteem.

AgeEsteem is learning from others who practice AgeEsteem.

MODELS FOR LIVING

The finest lessons are living examples.

PEOPLE WHO ARE MODELS OF AgeEsteem and the principles behind AgeEsteem® offer a valuable dimension to these pages. A number of these role models are older examples who show us how to live well at stages that are still far ahead of us. Some of them are peers or younger than I am. Each of them is an example of how we touch the lives of others and how we learn from others.

An important lesson of AgeEsteem is to emulate the positive traits we see in others as they deal with their own aging. We want to imprint those traits into our own lives. As babies we mimicked the people around us. We discovered how to walk and talk as a result of watching others and being encouraged by them. We continue to learn by example.

Many people who have positively influenced me have passed through my life in a matter of hours or minutes.

We each have our own choice of role models, people we seek to be like, who present an example of what we wish to become.

Some are world figures who have left a lasting mark on history. Many are present in the news, on the television or movie screen, or in images on billboards and advertising pages.

The vast majority, however, are the unsung heroes of our lives. They are women and men within our private circle of contacts. Not all will be part of a lasting relationship. Some of my most influential and remarkable life examples are people who have passed through my life in a matter of hours or minutes, but the impact remains and translates into many of my actions.

Within these pages are examples of seemingly ordinary people who are extraordinary role models of AgeEsteem. We can learn from their example.

CHAPTER 1

ADDING PIZZAZZ TO AGE

Adding a taste of pizzazz to life gives it a special zing.

The first step for growing AgeEsteem is to understand and accept that the concept of age is constantly evolving.

Of this we can be certain. Age just isn't what it used to be.

Shut your eyes for a moment and picture in your mind someone who is old. Go ahead. Shut your eyes and picture that old person.

What does that person look like? Describe her expression, posture, clothing and the overall impression she leaves with you. Keep this image in your mind as you read further.

No matter what your age is, chances are strong that you envisioned someone of your grandparents' generation. It is unlikely that you pictured someone your own age or even your parents' ages. You saw your grandmother or grandfather or one of their peers as they are today or as they were years ago.

When participants at AgeEsteem® presentations or workshops are asked that question 70% will picture a grandparent or someone of that same generation. Others tend to picture someone of their parents' era. Very few visualize a peer.

Aging is not what it used to be.

I was shocked by my own image of an older person when I first tried this. My grandparents popped into my mind looking as they did when they were in their 60's. I didn't picture my parents. My parents were not even old in their 80's. They were too engaged in life to age.

Whatever you envisioned, you will probably agree that age just isn't what it used to be. A person in her 70's today is more like the 50 year old of our grandparents' generation. We have improved through diet, activity, and overall health.

Today we are computer literate, drive sporty cars, climb mountains, play sports, win contests, and contribute in multiple ways through our work, talents and wisdom.

With people living longer and better lives, why are we still concerned about aging?

COMMUNICATION AND TECHNOLOGY

This concern is strongly influenced by the era of communication and technology in which we live. Today's media greatly dictates our perceptions of the world and of ourselves within that world. Media distorts our thinking and leads society to worship youth. Young is beautiful. Old is ugly. Everywhere we seem to be bombarded by products to help us look, act and feel young. Wrinkle erasers, diet patches, sexual enhancement pills, laser treatments, cosmetic surgery and hair transplants shout at us from advertisements every time we look at a bill board, open a magazine, or read the spam that sneaks through our e-mail.

Do these have value? Of course they do. But it's important to recognize the influence that they hold on us. The underlying message that is implicit behind these products is that youth is to be revered and age is to be fought. Youth is beautiful; age is ugly. Therefore, we have teenagers modelling for face creams on creaseless faces that have not even begun to show character. This leaves those of us who have lived and do have lines of expression to prove it feeling flawed.

Where in the media are the real scenes of our times? Where is the great-grandmother racing around in her red convertible? Where is the elderly man speaking on his cell phone while he jogs? Where are the seniors who are trekking in Peru? These are the real scenes that are pertinent to aging today.

We age with pizzazz. We are alive with passions and dreams and desires to make a positive, lasting difference.

We have pizzazz! We are alive with passions and dreams and desires to make a positive, lasting difference. Our lives continue to be full and exciting. We want to leave a legacy, a piece of ourselves for posterity but we also want to fully live while we are doing it.

Time is actually on our side. We are living longer and in better health.

In my constant research and testing for developing AgeEsteem, I visit multiple sites on the web. Several offer tests to determine your 'real' age. In other words, it measures, based on heredity, health, diet, exercise, and medical history, what your age is in relation to the life you live. While visiting one of the sites, I answered the questions. My curiosity was tickled. What would it tell me? Shortly after completing the questionnaire the answer flashed onto the screen. It indicated that based on the information I provided, I could anticipate living to be 95 years old.

Just think of what that means. It's telling me that I may still have over a third of my life ahead of me!

Statistics tell us that the average American woman can expect to live until the age of 80.5 years and the average man to the age of 75 years. But I'm no longer a statistic. This test tells me that I, Bonnie Fatio, can expect to live another half of the 60+ years I've already lived.

In my 60's, I am living the youth of my senior years.

It certainly puts my present age into a new perspective. If I am going to be here during the next 30 years, I better grow an attitude towards actively living those years. It's prime time to decide how I want to live and what I want to leave as my legacy to future generations.

OLDER AND BOLDER

Being in my 60's, I am living the youth of my senior years. And what is most attractive is that I can now stand in my own power. I no longer need to constantly prove myself. I know who I am and am comfortable with myself. I can now enjoy my age instead of constantly wishing I were older in order to have more credibility or to be permitted to do something. Today I give myself permission to do what I choose. I stand in my own power as a mature person.

My heritage of years of living makes me who I am today.

Even developing the concept and business of AgeEsteem is dependent on this maturity and the confidence and credibility that accompany it.

AgeEsteem® has grown out of my years of education, training, learning, growing, developing my skills and talents, mentoring, coaching, teaching; being bumped and bruised with lessons to be learned; reaching out to others; being carried through the worst of times by faith, friends and loved ones; jumping off the deep end to test the theory of swimming, racing into the future with complete abandon at some stages and with caution and trepidation at others; laboring to give birth.

It builds on experience encompassing family and friends with love, and accepting that they do the same for me. It includes being present with support and understanding even when I don't really understand or know how to support.

It includes painful injuries and illnesses; seeking answers to broken relationships and needless suffering; saying goodbye to loved ones; testing the force of resilience to move on and discover what else awaits me; overcoming doubts by giving them a name and delving ahead; realizing what a precious commodity friendship is; learning to put myself aside in order to concentrate on the healing or development of others; trusting my instincts and spirituality; knowing the comfort and release of tears and the joy and elation of laughter; welcoming new challenges even though they initially seem overwhelming; and the years spent emulating exceptional people who have contributed greatly to who I am.

This heritage of years of living makes me who I am today. This is what gives me the strength to stand in my own power and to realize the scope of what I can do for this next third of my life. What ever is to be is up to me. I can continue to grow and contribute further to the world, or I can sit back and watch from the sidelines.

I choose to welcome each new day and to decide how I will make the most of it. Age is not what it used to be!

The concept of age has changed and will continue to evolve. It's for each of us to decide how we want to make the most of these coming years and to continually enjoy the age we are.

AgeEsteem is recognizing that the concept of aging is evolving
and seniors can live with pizzazz.

THE HIDDEN IMAGE OF AGE

We carry our own back pack of images, language
and attitudes related to age and what it represents.

MUCH OF OUR RELATIONSHIP TO age is dependent on the image that age portrays for us. It is important to recognize what these images are in order to enhance, convert or abolish them.

Take five minutes right now to do a quick exercise. Rapidly write down every word that comes to mind when you think of age and older people. Write as many adjectives as possible as rapidly as you can without thinking about them.

Look at your list and highlight or underline those adjectives that are positive, the words that you feel good about. Don't be surprised if there are none or very few positive ones.

Now take the words that are not positive and ask yourself why you associate them with age. Are these words ageism stereotypes? Do they result from personal experience you or people around you have had?

A first step towards overcoming these negatives is to understand them.

We all have hidden biases concerning age. Interesting research concerning unconscious biases relating to old people and young people uses the Implicit Association Test (IAT). It is designed to detect biases that we do not even know we have. Regardless of what we consciously know to be correct, our cultural conditioning influences our subconscious. Our subconscious is constantly recording the multiple messages we hear and see. It never stops.

Research using IAT shows us that we are indeed biased against age. Studies show that among the strongest levels of bias are those directed against the elderly.

I experienced the IAT for myself by taking the test on-line. My data suggested a moderate automatic preference for 'Young' compared to 'Old'. In other words, I have a hidden bias toward youth even though I am consciously and overtly promoting age. In fact 80% of people who took this particular IAT on-line gave some degree of preference to young as opposed to old.

Let your AgeEsteem shine as a beacon to show others the way.

The next time you catch yourself using a negative adjective for aging, stop. We need to consciously perfect our own vocabulary and thoughts towards aging in order to influence the attitude within our society.

AgeEsteem is recognizing our own hidden image of age and modernizing it.

CHAPTER 2

FROM DOUBTS TO DREAMS AND DARING

Doubts are like bubbles. They take on a life of their own,
but when you face them head on they burst and make way for dreams.

do you have a dream in your heart today that you keep pushing aside? Do you let doubts about your own capabilities and self worth stand between you and what you want to do? Do you catch yourself thinking you're too old to take on something new?

Doubts and fears have to be met head on. We need to define what that doubt is and speak to it boldly. If we leave doubts alone they grow, but if we recognize them and call them by name they dissipate and disappear.

HOW DARE I?

The idea of AgeEsteem® had been buzzing in my brain for some time. I simply couldn't put it into words. Then it hit me. I was turning 60! Suddenly, age, A-G-E stared me in the face. "Oh, no," I thought. "Am I becoming one of them? One of the older generation?" My heart all but stopped beating as my stomach rolled over with a lurch and my body froze. The dreadful thought of moving into the camp of the elderly blew over me like the Artic wind. I shivered in the sunshine of my prime. My confidence and esteem shattered. I was entering a new decade, the Big Six Oh!

What was going on? I didn't feel 60. My personal image was certainly not that of my Grandmother at this golden age! I was still full of vitality and life.

During these 60 years I have learned that only I can overcome my fears. No one else can do it for me. As a result, when something scares me, I get acquainted with what is behind that fear. I identify it and get to know it intimately. Then I decide how to deal with it. This sudden fear of turning 60 was no different.

How dare I be 60! And how dare society and the press give me the impression that the best is behind me! Because that's exactly the image of aging that the media promotes when referring to older people. Aging, being older, is not a good thing. You've only to listen to the stereotypes used when referring to the "little old lady" or the "dinosaurs", to know that it's not a preferred segment of society.

This is our time to dream and to dare in order to realize our dreams.

I felt young at 60. I refused to accept these negative images of aging. I would become a catalyst for developing a new, dynamic image of aging and build excitement towards gathering years!

So I started visualizing how this should be – and the idea grew. And then grew some more, until it became a happy genie with a mind and soul of its own.

Then doubts set in. Big doubts.

How dare I believe that I could change these views? Who am I to do this? "I'm just an ordinary person", I told myself. Almost like magic as I began to express my doubts and fears, a voice boomed forth in my mind. "That is exactly why you should do it. If you do this, others are sure to join in. And they'll do it because you're not special. You're like each of them."

"Others have the same fears and concerns and challenges when it comes to growing older."

"If you can face these in positive ways, anyone can. If you can build your own new attitude towards aging drawing on your life experiences, anyone can."

"Not being exceptional is your force!"

And the bubbles of doubt began to burst one after the other.

My happy genie turned into a dream. I dream of age and aging being celebrated! I envision older people who are revered as important, contributing members of society. I see a movement that unleashes this positive image of aging and makes it the norm.

And I know it can be done!

The question of age touches everyone. We all want to be respected and recognized as valued members of our world.

It's time to burst any bubbles of doubt about ourselves due to age and to participate actively to improve our world.

This is our time to dream and to dare in order to realize those dreams.

What will you dare to do?

AgeEsteem is bursting any bubbles of doubt about myself due to my age.

LIVE YOUR AGE!

Give yourself permission!
Break out of your self-imposed barriers and try something new.

HOW WE IDENTIFY WITH AGE is internal. It is a state of mind. How we relate to age and how we feel about ourselves at the age we are today, as well as age in general, is internal. This is a measure of our AgeEsteem.

We are the age we feel ourselves to be. This could also be worded, "We are the age we allow ourselves to be."

Ask yourself. "Do I place barriers around myself? Do I forbid myself to live my life fully? Am I controlling my life too closely?"

People often say to me, "You're so lucky to be able to do that. I could never let myself do that at my age. What would people think?" They may be referring to the red suit I am wearing, the fact they saw me on a motorcycle, or simply that they caught me doing something silly. None of this is earthshaking. The sun will still rise tomorrow.

My reaction to them is, "Hey, wait a minute. Listen to what you're saying. You are admiring something I do. Yes, you are reacting positively saying you would like to do it too. So why wouldn't others react just as positively towards you if you allowed yourself to have fun, even be silly? They just might admire you for it."

Secondly, who cares what they think? Right, you do. You care what they think. I can understand this, so why not try the following.

Stretch through and beyond.

Think about something you would love to do but you hold yourself back because you're afraid of what others might think. Write down what it is you would like to do. Now think of the worst that could happen, the very worst, and write that also. Would you be arrested and thrown in prison? Not likely. Would you break a leg? Possibly, but it isn't probable. Would people laugh? Perhaps. Is it possible that nothing negative would happen? Most likely.

Now ask yourself, what is the best that could happen? The answer may seem simple and non consequential such as, "I will have a good laugh." It may also be something that will lead you to another level. For instance, if you want to take tango lessons maybe the best that could happen goes beyond just learning to dance. It could be that you would also meet new friends or eventually enter a tango competition.

Look at this experience as the first domino that sets off the reaction to spark a series of positive events. It just might create a chain reaction that makes your life even better.

Begin today. What's one limiting belief you have? Decide how you will break through it. What will you do concretely? What is your first step?

Breaking down your self-imposed barriers will lead to further confidence and you will feel more at ease as you continue to grow with each new experience.

AgeEsteem is knocking down self-imposed obstacles
and stretching beyond your previous limits.

WHAT WILL PEOPLE THINK?

To believe that you must act your age is to limit yourself greatly. What age? Defined by whom?

ON A RAINY DAY my daughter and I were walking home from school together when she suddenly tugged on my arm and asked, "Mom, why are people looking at us?" Only then did I realize that we were singing in the rain and twirling our umbrellas as we stomped through the puddles. What ever will people think?

Today, they would probably say, "She's having a senior moment." Well, if that is having a senior moment I say, "Let's have more of them!"

We are so programmed as to what is expected of us that when we do break the mold, we feel we are being courageous. "What will people think?" began haunting us as children and has followed us through life. Even now, when we should be enjoying more free time and the opportunity to do what we want, that nagging thought comes back, "What will people think?"

A favorite poem, *Warning*, which is better known as *When I am an Old Lady, I Shall Wear Purple*, by Jenny Joseph, makes numerous references to letting loose of restrictions and finally doing exactly what you want.

It is time to break out of habits and attitudes that stifle us and to burst through our own, self-imposed restrictions.

She's right to push us. Let's do more of what we enjoy, not less. If we want to wear purple or make a snowman or ride a scooter now is the time to do it. Why wait? Let's do it now! As long as it is socially acceptable, we can do anything we want.

Even the term *socially acceptable* doesn't have to be taken completely to heart. No, I don't recommend spitting on streets or shopping wearing only your underwear, but there is a huge span of possibilities between those and acting one's age. Look around us. What we think of as acceptable is, in many cases, archaic. Our children laugh at us when they see how we restrict ourselves to a convention that is no longer valid. Let's break the mold! Give ourselves permission!

It is time to break out of habits and attitudes that stifle us and to burst through our own, self-imposed restrictions. Let's put more music and color in life! Ring bells. Skip. Play. Dance with your walker. Clap your hands. Blow bubbles. Paint your cane. Whistle to the birds. Write love letters. Skate in the park. Cut and paste a photo collage. Knit a crazy patchwork quilt. Speak to a stranger. Wear scarlet socks. Eat ice cream in the street. Shuffle through the leaves. Create new activities. Compose new music. Build new furniture. Splash colors. Shock your friends. Sing in the rain!

There is a philosophy that I learned as a teacher which asserts that we learn best when we are in a state of confusion. Being confused is part of the learning process. We need to receive information and explanations and then process it all in our mind. This creates many thoughts and messages that bounce around in a confused state. This creates learning.

*Learning to stretch out of our comfort zone
allows us to test new boundaries.*

One of the best means of learning is to push yourself out of your comfort zone, to reach a point where you feel ill at ease. When you push yourself beyond the limits that you have experienced in the past, you test new boundaries. You discover that you can actually do more than you had thought. This allows you to learn further. And this extended limit becomes your new boundary. You have learned and moved beyond.

When we abandon our concerns about what others will think of us if we do something that doesn't fit into the norm for our age, what happens? If your response is that we feel uncomfortable or silly, you are probably right. But why do we feel silly? It's because we are pushing ourselves out of our comfort zone. We are stretching in new ways. We are experimenting and testing new possibilities. When we repeat something often enough it becomes normal. It's no longer unusual, uncomfortable or silly.

Not so long ago it was looked on as odd to wear bright colors if you were older than 40 or 50. Today most of us find it normal to wear colors we love at all ages. We don't wait to be old to wear purple nor do we avoid reds and yellows and bright blues as we age.

*Seniors must be active players in the economy,
politics and social platforms of our society.*

Let's go topsy-turvy and turn our world around. Let's feel free to do what we want. We have so much to offer to this world. We represent the accomplishments of the past but we also represent the challenges of the future. We must remain active players in the economy, politics and social platforms, active players who dream and dare.

What outrageous act will you commit today?

AgeEsteem is allowing yourself to do something courageous.

GLADYS

It's not because the majority is wrong
that you need to believe they are right.

GLADYS IS A GREAT ILLUSTRATION of someone who lives fully and follows her own standards.

I was immediately drawn to Gladys as she entered the room to attend an AgeEsteem® program in Colorado. She glowed with an inner beauty that comes from an excitement for life. Her white hair and red sweater were set off by her smile and sparkling eyes.

She introduced herself saying, "Do you know what makes me angry? It's people telling me what I should do." She continued, "Just because I'm 84, people think I should use a cane! I'm sick of hearing, 'Gladys, shouldn't you use a cane?'"

I later learned that Gladys had just walked three blocks through the snow because she felt it was safer than looking out for other drivers who don't drive well in the snow. Gladys is also a political economist and has her own blog. (Do you have your own blog?) She enjoys lecturing at a local university, belongs to the Wicked Widows exercise group and follows Tai Chi lessons.

As she was leaving after the workshop, she said, "Bonnie, I know what I'm going to do the next time someone tells me I need a cane. I'm going to say, "Cane! Yes, and let me get my top hat, too!'" And with that, she danced out the door.

AgeEsteem is living by your own standards.

PANIC! I FORGOT MY CODE

A major factor with memory is to believe you can remember.

MY FRIEND JULIE was in a complete panic. There she was at the automatic banking machine, and it had just indicated that the code she had typed was not valid. Surely she had not forgotten it. She must have touched the keys in the wrong sequence. Again she typed the numbers, but more slowly this time.   Once more that dreaded message flashed on the screen indicating that her code was incorrect. Was she losing her mind?

Julie knew that if she keyed in the wrong number a third time her card would disappear into the machine's bowels. It would take days to get her card back.   She raced into the bank in a complete panic.

Yes, it all worked out. She simply had inverted two of the numbers in her code, but the panic remained. Was she developing dementia? Was this the beginning of a future of forgotten numbers and names? She lives alone. What would happen when she could no longer remember her code to get money? Who would take care of her to remind her who she is? Fear took over and she began to doubt her own presence of mind.

These are scary moments and we need to deal with them. We need to be able to place these incidents into perspective. Forgetting your code does not have to mean that you are losing your mind.

Older people retain new knowledge as well as younger people.

How many times did I forget my keys or invert the numbers on the combination to my gym locker in High School? It happened numerous times, usually during exams when it was urgent to get into my locker rapidly. Did I panic? No, or at least not for the same reasons. Did I doubt my capacity to remember other things as a result? No.

There were times when we also made silly mistakes like pouring orange juice into our coffee cup or putting jelly on our cereal instead of on our toast in the morning. Did this trigger doubts about losing our minds? No. We just laughed and decided maybe that cup of coffee might help us wake up.

Once we are over 50 we anticipate that we will begin to forget, so when we do forget we wonder if it is the beginning of Alzheimer's or dementia. The same holds true when we do something silly such as pour juice into our coffee cup.

Think of your brain as a muscle that needs exercise like any other muscle. Learn something new each day.

There is much we can do to keep our minds alert and our memory alive. One major factor with being able to remember things is to believe that you can remember. When you do forget, tell yourself, "My mind is alert and I remember things easily." Rather than entertain doubts, relax and focus.

BLUEBERRIES

Dr. Ann Kato, a professor of neuroscience at the University of Geneva who has extensively researched brain rejuvenation, insists that people in good health are completely capable of learning at any age. Older people retain knowledge as well as younger people do.

Dr. Kato offers simple remedies for keeping your mind healthy.

1. Eat lots of blueberries. Blueberries is the food that has the greatest positive effect on the brain. It does not really matter if the blueberries are fresh or whether they are frozen, but they must have the skin on them.

2. Walk 10,000 steps per day. Walk whenever and wherever you can. Purchase a pedometer to measure how many steps you take. Measuring our steps helps us to consciously increase the number of steps we take each day.

3. Exercise your brain. Learn something new. Play games that challenge your thinking such as bridge or chess. Work on crossword puzzles, logic problems or Su-do-ku. Any exercise that makes you think is a good one.

Did you forget something? Don't panic. Put the incident into perspective and remind yourself that your memory is intact.

AgeEsteem is exercising your brain to keep it healthy.

YOU WERE WONDERFUL, RICHARD!

Sing, laugh and dance everyday, even if only in spirit.

RICHARD DOESN'T KNOW IT. HE wasn't even there, but he was truly wonderful!

When I told my guests that he'd agreed to sing for my 60th if I were willing to dance, they went wild. Imagine. Richard Gere singing at your birthday!

Of course, it did mean that I had to dance, but after seeing the film *Chicago*, my feet were moving before I even found a dance instructor.

Seeing Richard in that movie pushed me to realize a childhood dream. Learning to tap dance.

To realize a dream, you must begin to act on it.

Ever since I was little, the sound and movement of tap dancing have fascinated me. Two of my strong values are freedom and fun. Both describe tap dancing. Did you notice how Richard constantly smiled while he danced? The music and dancing in *Chicago* was a lark for him.

As I told the guests, there's something special about turning 60! It's the perfect time to look one's dreams in the face.

As a child, I ended up in ballet class despite the teacher's prompt evaluation that I had the grace of a wild boar and would never become a star. My one moment of glory was in the *Nutcracker Suite*, marching as a tin soldier.

It was also understood from my mother that "good girls don't tap dance." This probably added to its glamour since I had no idea what "bad girls" did while tapping. If tap dancing was part of being bad, I wasn't so sure I wanted to be good.

Think of a spider web holding sparkling jewels of morning dew,
and know that nothing is impossible.

Shortly after seeing Richard dance in *Chicago* for the second time, I decided that I'd learn to tap dance. I'd dance at my 60th as a gift to my sisters.

Within days I began lessons in a class where no one was under the age of 35. It was perfect. I needed neither to wear a tutu nor to try to look svelte in a fuchsia leotard. And it became even better. When the instructor learned that I wanted to actually perform for others within eight weeks, she set a private weekly session to create the choreography and teach me the steps.

Our first challenge was to set up some kind of dance floor in our apartment for lessons and practice. My husband, the engineer, quickly remedied this. For a party, he'd built two large, round table tops that folded. They were ideal. One for the instructor. One for me. They had just the right resonance, making the taps almost musical. And, I'm now able to say that I began my dancing career on tabletops!

My 60th arrived and my dream came true. While Richard sang *Razzle Dazzle*, on the CD, I danced. Did we take the guests by surprise! When Richard broke into song, and I into dance, they yelled and whistled with delight. In fact, when half way through I clicked my heels in the air, they were so loudly enthusiastic that I couldn't hear the music - and Richard and I had to begin again. Nothing like having an early encore!

Thank you, Richard. You were wonderful! But what's even more wonderful is that I don't need you anymore.

Richard helped me to realize this dream of learning to tap dance and to perform for others, but now I don't need him for my new dream.

Here I am. Doing it on my own!

What is your dream?

AgeEsteem is knowing it is never too late to realize our dreams.

CHAPTER 3
ALWAYS PRESENT IN MY LIFE

I WANT TO BE ME

"Being me" provides a liberating force
that makes it possible to stand out in meaningful ways.

One of my favorite cartoons shows a multitude of penguins on a mountain of ice. As handsome as they are in their little tuxedos, they all look alike. So many penguins are cramped together that you see nothing but the tops of their look-alike bodies. Standing out in the middle of them is one penguin waving his fin and singing, "I want to be me!"

Celebrate who you are.

We all want to stand out in some special way. We want to be recognized as individuals with separate identities and personalities. Each of us wants to "be me".

Few of us have consciously questioned ourselves about what we want that identity to be. Instead, we have naturally fallen into various roles that bring their own identity such as parent, spouse, volunteer and professional.

Each of us measures ourselves against someone or something else: the success of our children and spouse; whether we got promoted at work; the kind of car we drive. Advertising, television programs, movie stars, even dolls have a crucial impact on how we see ourselves. They continually program us to think that unless we act and look a certain way or use a particular product, we are of lesser value to society.

Aging makes us prime targets for these messages. My friend Joan says, "The industries 'use' older people. Advertisers persecute us with their messages. They create a consumer need by making us feel less attractive and less valuable if we don't comply with the image of youth that only their products can offer. It's difficult to combat this and to feel whole."

What these products cannot give us is beauty that exudes from an internal glow of excitement and zest for life. This is the beauty that comes from within, from knowing who you are and being confident in your own image. This inner glow comes from practicing AgeEsteem.

YOU have the power to BE YOU.

It is up to you to define for yourself who you are and what you want to contribute to others now that the children have left home, retirement is on the horizon, or you seek to build more personal meaning into your life. Life expectancy becomes greater each year that we live. Now is a good time to begin to "be me" for the rest of your life.

There is only one person who can do this – you.

The messages in these pages will help you. Stop and reflect about yourself in different ways as you read this book, and test its concepts. Use it to define yourself.

Once we recognize ourselves as unique personalities with specific qualities, we can define how to best share those qualities.

To accept yourself as the unique person you are means to recognize your individual personality and special qualities, interests and values. Only then can you define how to best share those qualities. This identity, this "being me", is the liberating force that makes it possible to stand out in ways that are meaningful to you. Accepting your own uniqueness enables you to accept others with their uniqueness.

Start now by reaching out to others. Stretch towards new horizons. Embrace your dreams. Magnify your visions. Know that YOU control your thoughts. YOU have the power to BE YOU.

AgeEsteem is recognizing and expressing your uniqueness.

CREATING A LIFE WITH PURPOSE

The choice is mine.

WHAT DISTINGUISHES THE HUMAN RACE from other species is the fact that we make conscious choices.

We control our lives through these choices, however great or small those choices may be.

Think about it. Every action that we take is our choice. The way we view what happens in our lives is our choice. This is a very powerful ability. Yet we forget that the choices are ours to make. Even deciding that you do not have the power to choose is a choice.

Many choices are made out of habit. I don't need to consciously choose which route to take home from work. I do it every day, but the choice is still there. Even though we are caught up in a habit, we can change.

To have a purposeful life, we need to assume responsibility and to take action. Both depend on making choices. Both come from within us. Age may modify some of the choices that we make, just as being young once limited our choices of the moment. We do have choices, however. We can decide to take responsibility, to own what we do.

We can then choose to act on our choice. A decision without action is sterile. It leaves us with the impression that we are caught in a snow storm and can no longer see where we want to go.

How I age is dependent on how I choose to live.

How we age is a choice. It is up to us to decide what attitude we wish to adopt and how we wish to act. We can greet each new day with enthusiasm and plans, or we can drag ourselves through the day listening to our own complaints.

Personally, I prefer the former. It's much more enjoyable to treat the day as a gift to be opened with anticipation.

Interesting research includes the study of older people who define their lives as happy and meaningful. The reports of several studies that I read show that these people live longer. What is equally interesting is that their joy in living is not related to a painless body. They live with the same amount of physical discomforts as others in the same age group. They simply choose to focus on what is interesting in life and to find purpose, their *raison d'être*. They choose to take responsibility for their own happiness and to act.

Think about the following questions. Let them provoke you. There is no correct or incorrect answer. These are personal questions which only you can answer.

* What is your purpose/mission/vision for your life?
* What is your goal for today?
* What talents, skills and qualities do you have to share?
* How would you like to share them?

❋ With whom would you like to share them? If you don't think you
have anyone with whom to share, go to the chapter Building Support.

Start gently and build a rhythm.

As you develop your purpose in new ways, ask yourself how this has
increased your personal power.

AgeEsteem is taking responsibility for your choices and acting on them.

GLOW IN YOUR TALENTS

Our greatest challenge with aging is
to continue to live up to our own potential.

DO YOU ALLOW YOUR PERCEPTION of aging to influence the way you express your talents and potential?

During AgeEsteem® presentations I ask participants to introduce themselves to as many of the other people as possible by simply stating their name and age.

As simple as it may sound, for many this begins as a difficult task. It isn't natural to spontaneously reveal our age. A real concern is "What will others think when they know my age?"

The way others see us is not necessarily how we see ourselves.

After a workshop, Alexandra visited me to explain her new lease on life. It began with that exercise.

"When you asked us to introduce ourselves to the others in the room stating our age, I was horrified. I could barely get the words out. And I felt flattered when someone said, '74? You don't look that old!'"

"It started me thinking that maybe others didn't see me as the older person I thought I was."

"Later, when you asked us to write down what we have to offer today as opposed to just one year ago, I began to think about aging differently. I <u>do</u> have talents that continue to develop and I know I have a need to share them. My dissatisfaction with age has really been discomfort because my creative instincts were smothered. And this was because I felt I was no longer relevant. It actually was my attitude towards age that became a wall between me and what I love to do most and do best."

Alexandra is a jewel of creativity. What she does with rhyming words and drawing crazy caricatures on cards for friends is amazing. She is a creative wizard with words and drawings, yet she had forgotten that this is true. She had fallen into thinking, "I'm too old to…" As a result she hid her precious talent. She continued to age, but forgot to LIVE. Today she glows through the use of her talents.

Why not follow her example? Begin now!

Many talents develop out of the experience of living.
They become richer with age.

Perhaps you are a great cook, speaker or sailor. Maybe you have a knack for making people feel at ease or solving problems, telling stories or playing the accordion.

Remind yourself what your special qualities are. Look at what you have loved to do and have been recognized for in the past. Make a list. It may take time to rediscover some of these special assets. That's fine. Add to your list as more talents come to mind. Remind yourself of what you know today because you are more experienced than yesterday. Your talents become richer with each day you live.

AgeEsteem is glowing in your talents.

PERSONAL TALK

The ripple effect of positive self-talk travels on and on and on.

RESEARCH IN COGNITIVE PSYCHOLOGY, THE study of how our minds function, teaches us that messages we send to ourselves influence how we live. The way that we talk to ourselves, the thoughts that run through our minds, affect how we relate to different situations.

Let's take the example of moving to a new home because your present home is too big. You just don't need so much space, and it is difficult to maintain it. Perhaps you're moving where health care is available.

How you think about it in your mind, the way you speak to yourself, will be crucial to settling happily into your new home.

Our thoughts affect how we live.

A person who focuses on the positive aspects of the change will adjust to the experience more easily. "This home has served us well over the years. I will carry a multitude of happy memories of our times here. I am thankful that I've been able to keep it all these years." And "This new home offers many activities with other people. I know I'll make interesting new friends. I look forward to living where health care is easily accessible. I'm pleased that my children will not worry about me." These are messages that can facilitate the transition and adaptation to new surroundings.

TRAIN YOUR BRAIN

Train your brain to focus on positive self-talk. For one week keep a diary, and record what you tell yourself. Note what the circumstances are. Are you afraid, excited, pleased? Do you feel that you have lost control of a situation? Are you lonely, angry or feeling depressed? Happy or energized? Listen to what you say to yourself and write it down.

Train your brain to focus on positive self-talk.

Once you have written down what you actually said, change any negative statement into a positive one. Speak these positive words out loud. Any time you catch yourself repeating a negative message, immediately replace it with a positive one again. Continue doing this until the up-beat messages completely dominate your self-talk.

For example, "I'm having a senior moment." becomes "I remember easily."

"I'm too old for that." can become "I can do anything that I set my mind to."

Make this Personal Talk Diary your own. Use whatever style you prefer. It can be telegraphic style, long paragraphs, two-liners or mind-mapping.

The importance is to keep a record and to actively change the negative thoughts into positive ones.

As our personal talk becomes positive our confidence increases.

When you become aware of your language and speak positively to yourself, you will feel happier and more confident as you focus on the brighter side of life. Little by little you will become an expert at speaking to yourself positively.

Other people will begin to find you more attractive and interesting as you practice this new skill. When your personal talk becomes positive it affects how you feel about yourself and your environment. You gain more confidence. By focusing on positives you draw other positive energy to you.

AgeEsteem is training our minds to focus on powerful positive thoughts.

BUILDING EXCITEMENT

Enhance your strongest talents
to become a champion in what you do best.

WHAT MOTIVATES YOU? WHAT IS your passion in life? What
do you love to do most?

Live with passion.

A technique for living well and having energy is to do what you love.
When we are motivated by what we do, we feel good. Our energy level
is higher. We get caught up in what we are doing with enthusiasm. We
become oblivious to time. We even forget our aches and pains when we are
involved in something that gives us pleasure.

Why, then, do we forget to focus on what we enjoy doing and do well?

As a motivational coach, I have worked with hundreds of people who
have lost track of what matters to them as individuals. They got so caught
up in their work that they did not even realize that they no longer enjoyed
what they were doing.

Usually we are good at a job because we like it. It allows us to use our
talents and the training that we followed because we were motivated by
what we could do with the training.

What I see happen time and time again is that we allow ourselves to be pulled away from what we enjoy. Because we are good at what we do, we are considered for promotion and move up the ladder. This goes on until one day we wake up and ask, "What am I doing here? I used to love my job. Now I have trouble dragging myself out of bed!"

I refer to this as the Bonnie Principle. It's similar to the Peter Principle which says that you will continue to get pushed ahead on the job until you are no longer competent. The Bonnie Principle says that you will get pushed into new situations and new jobs until you are pushed out of your energy zone. You may well be competent, but you have lost interest. The activities of the job no longer motivate you.

Offer yourself the luxury of exploring your motivations.

The cure for this can be simple. Get back in touch with what motivates you. Take a serious look at these motivators and ask yourself, "How can I build them back into my life? How can I redesign my way of working and living to utilize these motivators more fully?"

These questions are equally critical when we experience transitions such as children leaving home, the death of a parent or retiring from a job. Each of these represents major activities and defines our identity.

Offer yourself the luxury of exploring your motivations. Start by setting quality time aside to renew your own acquaintance. Look at your life from several perspectives as though you are viewing yourself from various angles through different camera lens.

Think back over the times in your life that you were happiest. These may not have been major events. They may be the quiet moments that were special for you, or particular periods in your life. Look at these through the lens of this imaginary camera in your mind and describe the scene.

For each snap shot look at the activity you are involved in. Is it intellectual, physical, technical? Who are the people around you? Are they old friends, strangers, family members? Are you alone? What are you doing? Are you building, creating, following directions, taking a risk, entertaining? What is the setting? Are you outdoors, on a mountain, in your bed, in a theater? Ask yourself as many questions as possible to pin point what the motivating factors are.

Now go back and answer the question, "What do I like about this activity? How do I like to accomplish it?" In other words, describe why the activity motivates you and under what conditions.

A key to longevity is to do what you love, and love what you do.

Our goal is to learn from these past events in order to build more satisfaction and pleasure into our present lives. Redefining yourself in this way by who you are, what matters to you, what you value, and what you love to do most, opens doors that you may have long forgotten. Being aware of what motivates you enables you to emphasize these motivators again. As you build them into your activities, you will discover that you have more energy and pleasure.

* ❋ When we do what we enjoy, we become good at it.
* ❋ This increases our confidence, which transfuses all aspects of our life.
* ❋ People like to be around motivated, happy people. Others are drawn to us and like to help us succeed in our efforts.
* ❋ Being motivated by what we do keeps us healthier. We have fewer illnesses.
* ❋ We live longer.

Once you have built your motivators back into your life, here is a powerful technique you can use to keep sight of them. At the end of each day ask yourself, "What did I enjoy most today?" You can then decide how to build more of these positives into your life. You are in control.

The bonus benefit of this simple exercise is that it directs you to concentrate on the positives of today and to already plan for tomorrow to be a wonderful day.

AgeEsteem is recognizing what motivates you
and using your motivators lavishly.

IS YOUR ATTITUDE SHOWING?

I have full power over my attitude, no matter what the situation.

FOLLOWING A KNEE OPERATION I was sent to a clinic with thermal baths to accelerate the mending process. One of the daily exercises was aqua jogging in a pool.

As we ran through the deep water, bodies of the other patients were hidden. Only their heads were visible above the water.

What captured my attention were the facial expressions. People were ageless except for what I could interpret from the attitudes on their faces. Their bodies were invisible, their hair was wet and any makeup had long since washed away. Only the emotions and attitudes expressed on their faces showed any indication of age.

Are you proud to have your attitude show?

The joggers who fought the exercise and concentrated on their pain seemed older. Their faces were disfigured by pain, increased by their anger and displeasure.

Others who wore expressions of determination reminded me of children learning to ride a bike or complete a puzzle.

Those wearing an attitude of enjoying the effort showed the radiance that we associate with youth. They exuded confidence.

The aqua joggers who smiled with encouragement to others communicated a feeling of empathy. It was difficult to capture the movement to jog through the water.

Others found humor in the situation as they ran through the water in wet suits which could best be described as huge rubber shorts with a bib both in front and behind.

Our inner spirit must be in sync with what we wish to portray on the surface.

These facial expressions taught me a lesson. We may dress in sharp clothes and use make up to hide wrinkles; but unless our attitude complements the outer image, the attire is not complete and our desired message does not succeed. We must be congruent. Our inner spirit must be in sync with what we portray on the surface.

We are who we feel ourselves to be.

When, like the aqua joggers who exude an inner glow, we decide to make the most of what life brings our way and to enjoy the moment, years lose their importance. Our AgeEsteem is whole because we have confidence and integrity in our way of being. AgeEsteem combines how we feel about ourselves with what we wish to project to others. We are who we feel ourselves to be.

AgeEsteem is having our inner attitude congruent with our outer image.

BUBBLES AND KISSES

To see diamonds twinkling in the night sky is enough
to keep me believing in miracles.

WINNIE THE POOH IS A wonderful teacher. He calls himself a "bear of little brain." However, he's also a "bear of big heart." We can learn from his philosophy of life.

Each morning as Pooh awakens, he greets the day asking, "Ho. Hum. I wonder what great thing will happen to me today." As a result, he bounces out of bed in anticipation.

The truly wonderful outcome of seeking the miracle in each day
is that we not only find them. We create them!

A friend of mine, Roger, has a similar approach to life. It's to seek the miracle that each new day brings.

Every day becomes a new adventure!

It becomes a treasure hunt as he seeks that special pearl in his oyster, the retirement home where he lives. Sometimes his pearl is simply there and easily identified. Often he must open all of his senses to recognize it when it appears.

His miracles take the form of an unexpected telephone call or a visit from someone he cares about. They take the shape of meeting someone new, watching a stunning sunset, having a bird sing outside his window or a child reach for his hand.

The truly wonderful outcome of seeking the miracle in each day is that we not only find them. We create them!

My friend also likes to cause miracles. He tells the story of the woman who serves the coffee in the dining room. Often in a hurry, she pours the coffee rapidly. This causes bubbles to form. My friend has named these "love bubbles." As a result, the racing waitress now stops to see whether she created bubbles in his coffee. When there are none, she leans down to kiss his cheek and says, "Love isn't always bubbles."

Bubbles and kisses. Both become miracles in this man's day.

Take time to smell the miniature roses that line your path.

Miracles don't need to shake the earth. They need only to warm your heart, to help you relate to the world around you, and to remind you of what really matters.

Embrace them for what they are: blessings and moments of joy!

What will be your miracle today?

AgeEsteem is seeking bubbles and kisses.

CHAPTER 4

JUST LET GO

Letting go enables us to enrich our lives in new ways.

etting go of what we do not need or that weighs us down liberates us. It sets us free.

An important aspect of AgeEsteem is to be oriented towards the future. But to move forward freely into the future also means getting rid of excess baggage.

It is like flying in a hot air balloon that is propelled by the wind. When Bertrand Picard and Brian Jones piloted the Breitling Orbiter 3 balloon in 1999 to circle the world, they managed to keep their balloon airborne for 20 days and 26,600 miles. The only means they had to direct their balloon was to discharge ballast. Lightening their load allowed them to rise to capture winds that carried them to their goal.

Life is also like this. In order to embrace the future and continue to make meaningful contributions, we also must discharge ballast. This may be in the form of material objects, hard feelings, pain or broken relationships. They represent the weight on our balloon of life.

It requires both desire and commitment to change and let go.

Only we can direct our balloon and decide to discharge this excess ballast. The decision is ours. We are in control. This control includes deciding to leave thoughts, things, and people behind us.

Whether we do this progressively or abruptly, it requires us to have the desire and to make a commitment to change.

An important aspect of letting go for us today is to let go of inhibitions and limiting beliefs about aging.

How often do you catch yourself thinking, "I'm too old for that"? Do you say this even when you're eager to try something new or something you did when you were younger? Believing that you are too old is a limiting belief. It stunts your pleasure in life.

An important aspect of letting go is to shed your inhibitions and limiting beliefs about age and aging.

Replace these limiting beliefs with "can do - will do" beliefs. If you catch yourself thinking you're too old to learn to play the piano, counteract that statement. Remind yourself that you enjoy music, you learn rapidly and you are manually dexterous. Then state an action to get started. "I can find a teacher. I will begin lessons." It's only once you have begun lessons that you will know what talent you have. And that talent is not dependent on age. A bonus will be actively exercising your fingers and your mind. This will keep both your finger joints and brain cells healthy.

Letting go allows us to

* ✻ Remove clutter from our lives.
* ✻ Forgive, forget, and move on.
* ✻ Break loose from self-imposed barriers.
* ✻ Free energy for future oriented activities.
* ✻ Discover new opportunities.

Lighten your life in order to strengthen your AgeEsteem.

AgeEsteem is letting go of inhibitions
and personal limiting beliefs about age.

SHIFTING GEARS

When we let go, we liberate ourselves to
move on to other things and to develop in new ways.

ONE OF MY GREATEST LESSONS in life was imposed on me in a way I would never have chosen. It came in the form of an accident that put me flat on my back for two months.

The day began like many others. I had driven our daughter to school, where I also worked. Racing between buildings and appointments I slipped on the ice and couldn't get up. When I opened my eyes, there was a little boy next to me asking, "Are you dead?" "Good news", I thought. "I'm definitely still alive." But I couldn't get up. I had crushed vertebrae. Fortunately no lasting damage was done, but this super woman, wife, mother and professional, was no longer able to control everything.

I had to psychologically shift gears and learn to let go.

First was to let go of my independence. I had to learn to let others take care of me and to do for me. When I let go of this independence and control, something wonderful happened. I began to understand the pleasure it gave others to do something for me. And I began to enjoy it too.

When I let go of this independence and control, I began to understand
the pleasure it gave others to do something for me.

A favorite example was the day Laetitita, our then 9 year old daughter who had already made me designs and games, asked me if there was something else she could do for me. I suggested, "Yes. Do you think you could get out my jewelry box and arrange my jewelry for me?" This turned into a magical memory that I have captured in my mind forever. Laetitia spent the next hour lovingly admiring and modelling each piece of jewelry before arranging them in the velvet box. The light in her eyes and the joy she shared, doing this for Mommy, is an image I treasure.

Secondly I had to let go of the thought that only I could fill my job effectively. Life went on at work without me.

Thirdly was to let go of being the giver and to learn to enjoy receiving. I was awed by the number of people who showed their concern and caring through gifts, flowers and notes. The greatest present they offered me, though, was to teach me to develop my empathy and understanding of others in a new way, helping me to be more effective in my relationships. But I had to let go of something within me for this to happen.

You have to let go in order to move forward.

This has been one of life's great lessons. You have to shift gears and let go in order to move forward. This may be in the form of letting go of anger, or envy, or the feeling that I must do everything myself.

It's possible that this becomes even more important as we mature and age. We may not be able to do as much as we used to. We may have to accept that others help us. But it does not mean that we are giving up. It means that we are letting go. There is a difference. When we let go, we are able to let go of a weight, which liberates us and allows us to move on to other things and to develop in new ways.

Do you remember when you first let go of the side of the pool in order to swim? Or let go of the learner wheels to ride your bike? Or let go of a monthly pay check? Or of a loved one who was ready to move on without you? I do. And through each experience I have been pushed to new heights of understanding, new opportunities for learning and new achievements.

Letting go enables us to enrich our lives in new ways.

What will you let go today?

AgeEsteem is learning to shift gears and to let go.

ONLY I CAN MAKE THE CHANGE

You are the only person alive who has sole custody of your life.

IN 1995 I EXPERIENCED A heart attack. I say experienced because it is not just a moment in time. It is an experience that influences how you live the rest of your life. When the first pain came I was sitting with a friend. Seeing the pain on my face, she asked me if I was all right. I said, "I think I may be having a heart attack." And we both burst out laughing. It was a ludicrous idea. After all, I was the image of good health.

It was several days later on vacation in another country with my family that I decided that something was seriously wrong. Even then the doctor found nothing to indicate a heart problem until I entered the hospital for further tests. It then became evident that I had indeed had a heart attack. Fortunately this problem does not have to recur.

I will live to LIVE.

This experience brought two important revelations. First was to face my own mortality and to realize that I felt comfortable with it. Death does not frighten me. I plan to live as long as possible in good health.

I will live to LIVE, not to avoid dying.

Secondly, I no longer needed to try to change everyone I met. I had felt it was my duty to try to change the attitude of the gruff bank clerk, cranky bus driver or pouting salesclerk. Today I no longer allow negative people within my space. Now I build on the positive within me and around me. I contribute my energy to constructive purposes.

I'm thankful for my heart attack, as painful as that time was, because it triggered a new approach to life. I still want everyone to be happy and feel good about themselves, but I've let go of the idea that it is up to me. They must change themselves.

Letting go of that idea has freed me to fly with the eagles. Everywhere I turn there are positive people who seem to be waiting for me to share their path. Positive energy attracts other good energy.

I build on the positive within me and around me.

Positive energy attracts other good energy.

Each of us is constantly letting go of something in our lives. We let go of our children a little each day as they grow. Often it is not until the day that they leave home to test their talents on their own, however, that we recognize this. For many this comes as a shock. We knew even before they were born that if we were successful parents they would leave us. But we were so wrapped up in the process of raising them, that somewhere along the line we forgot our own identity beyond that of being a parent.

Many of the experiences that push us to let go of what was, and to look towards what could be, come with age.

Tom, who took a professional class with me, lost his job when his company merged with another. He had been loyal to the company for 28 years, which was most of his career. Now, from one day to the next he found himself without a job, without a title, without a pay check, and seemingly without an identity.

Barbara, another of my professional friends, felt the same loss of identity when she retired. Her confidence and self esteem took a beating. People no longer sought her advice. There were no urgent deadlines, meetings to prepare, budgets, camaraderie in the hallways or endless communications. Unless she counted a dentist appointment and purchasing groceries, her agenda was blank. She felt old and unneeded.

Letting go of what is past allows us to embrace the future.

In each of these circumstances, there was a period of grief. They had lost something dear. But then the time came to say goodbye to the past and seek new opportunities to bloom and flourish. Before anything else could happen, though, they needed to let go of their loss.

An important aspect of letting go and looking forward is to decide what we want for our own lives. It is to say good bye to the past and to seek new opportunities to build our interests and talents.

Refer to the chapters *Building Excitement* and *Creating A Life With Purpose* to begin developing your AgeEsteem through new interests, dreams and action today.

AgeEsteem is letting go of what we cannot change and focusing on developing our interests.

GOOD BYE TREASURES

The fact of the matter is that we can't take it with us.

DO YOU HAVE TOO MUCH stuff but can't find the time to weed through it all? Are there objects and books that you had forgotten you owned, yet you can't bring yourself to give them away? It seems that we acquire more things every year.

Research shows that when we live in clutter, our lives get cluttered. When we clean out the clutter, we are better able to organize our lives as well as our homes.

When we let go of the excess we are better able to organize our lives as well as our homes.

It isn't always easy to give away objects that represent parts of our lives. But it isn't any fun to dust them, either. My husband and I were fortunate to inherit a number of lovely knick knacks and treasures, but the fact of the matter is that we have too much. Shelves are either cluttered or they are showing a small sample of what can be found in closets. I used to tell myself that we couldn't give them away while the older generation was still alive. After all, they were the ones who gave them to us. Nor do I want to sell them. They have been in the family for generations. So what to do?

Monica has given her precious books and articles to museums who were delighted to add them to their collections. Julien sold many of his heirlooms on eBay. It opened up a whole new hobby to him.

One friend of ours, Emma, has dedicated a floor of her place in the mountains to serve as a family museum. Do you have a treasure you don't want to keep? Give it to Emma. She'll put it on display. It will be the new discovery at the next family gathering.

Not all of us have this option. But there are other options. Sell it. Throw it out. Give it away.

Offer your treasures to others now to enjoy the pleasure of the giving.

Yvette was a champion at giving her extras away. She offered her treasures as birthday gifts, Christmas presents, and for weddings, baptisms and "just because". At family gatherings she organized games and quizzes. The winner would choose a prize from among her treasures. Once she invited all her grandchildren and gave each of them a number. When their number was drawn they could pick what they wanted. From a 12 room house she pared everything down to fit into a small apartment. When she died, there was very little to distribute. She had done the giving herself and had witnessed the joy and satisfaction her personal gifts brought to those she loved.

If you feel life is cluttered and you have too many things, why not try to throw out, sell or give away one object at a time? If you think of someone who might appreciate the object, put their name on it. You can offer it as a gift the next time you see them or save it for their birthday.   Deciding on the future of one article at a time can even be fun.

What treasure will you give away today?

AgeEsteem is getting rid of clutter and giving away treasures.

CHAPTER 5

CELEBRATE!

To celebrate life is to celebrate aging.

i grew up in a family where any occasion to celebrate was a good one. Birthdays, including those of pets, and holidays were full of decorations, surprises and laughter.

My father was a Methodist minister and we moved to a new city and school every four years. Looking back I realize it might have been a devastating experience. We regularly left friends and familiarity behind as we moved once again.

Celebration serves as a rite of passage during transitions.

Thanks to our love of celebration and my parents' talent to create advance excitement towards our new home, we anticipated each move as an adventure. Each time we were uprooted there were festivities to send us off. When we arrived at our new home there was a welcoming committee to help us again take root. Celebrations facilitated our transition from one community to the next.

During my career when my job was made redundant, even then I left with popping corks. My last day turned into a festive event that recognized what my colleagues and I had accomplished together. It focused us on the future as we acknowledged past accomplishments and turned the page.

When in doubt, celebrate! What great advice this is. To celebrate is to honor someone, something or a special day. It's positive. In the above examples, it becomes a rite of passage from one identity to the next.

Celebrating benefits our confidence, AgeEsteem and health.

We should celebrate lavishly as we age. The benefits to our confidence, AgeEsteem and health are multiple.

Celebrations

* Create positive energy.
* Help us concentrate on what is good and right and happy.
* Bring us together with others in a social atmosphere.
* Provide an excellent occasion to work in a team.
* Keep our minds alert as we plan and play.
* Generate laughter.
* Present opportunities to learn.
* Build our network of relationships.
* Allow us to shine through our talents.
* Stimulate our confidence.

❋ Often force us out of our comfort zone to test new skills in a friendly atmosphere.

❋ Are fun.

Looking at this list of benefits it's a wonder that physicians don't prescribe a regular dose of celebration to keep us healthy.

What will you celebrate?

AgeEsteem is celebrating often.

KEEPING MY FACE TOWARD THE SUN

Smile at yourself in the mirror and watch the glow begin.

IT WAS ALWAYS A MYSTERY to me. How does a sunflower manage to continually face the sun?

There's a back road I often choose during the summer months in order to admire fields of sunflowers en route to and from work. Whether it's early morning, late afternoon or evening, the flowers stand like an army of soldiers saluting the sun and basking in its rays. Even when the rays fade, the sunflowers continue to smile at the sun.

Someone finally explained to me that the neck of a sunflower is so flexible that it pivots as though on a ball bearing. Instead of twisting its long stalk, it simply rolls its agile neck to follow the sun.

Oh, to be a sunflower!

It's my own frame of mind that will decide how I greet the day.

Figuratively we are able to do the same. We, too, can be agile and flexible enough to keep facing the sun, if only in our thoughts. It's like looking at the sky and seeing either the little patch of blue or the mass of hovering clouds. It's our own attitude that will decide how we greet the day and all that it brings.

Are we looking for the blue or are we looking for the grey? Will we, too, manage to turn our faces towards the lighter side of the day, even though the sun seems to skip behind dark clouds?

I too can keep facing the sun, if only in my thoughts.

The answer is "Yes". Just as the sunflower smiles at the sun, so can we share optimism and faith that this will be a great day. We, too, can keep our faces to the sunny side of life and share our smile generously with others. We can share our confidence and optimism in life, our AgeEsteem.

Happiness is right in front of us. We need only to keep our face to the sun.

AgeEsteem is keeping your thoughts sunny
and sharing your smile generously.

LAUGHTER: THE BEST MEDICINE

Great laughter each day keeps the doctor away.

LAUGHTER IS A WONDERFUL GIFT that you can easily share with others. It's free and readily accessible. It also contributes toward feeling healthy and vital. It is a great booster shot for aging actively and well.

If ever you see someone without a smile, give him one of yours.

Can you remember being somewhere when someone started laughing and couldn't stop? Your own thoughts may have gone through instant gymnastics wondering what was so funny and why, until you became completely caught up in the laughter yourself. Probably along with many others.

The laughter was infectious and probably spread a feeling of good will. It lightened the atmosphere and created a moment of intimacy among strangers.

Laughter lightens the atmosphere and creates
a bond of intimacy among strangers.

We feel good when we laugh. It is not surprising that it is a terrific boost to good health. Researchers also have found that after laughing there is an increase in antibodies which are believed to have a capacity to protect us against some viruses and infections. It also reduces high blood pressure.

I've noticed in my own life that laughter alleviates pain. Whether it's physical or psychological pain, having a reason to laugh focuses our minds onto something funny and light. We forget the pain. This was true for me even when I had broken ribs. The doctor jokingly told me not to watch any funny movies because it would hurt to laugh. Holding my sides while watching funny movies actually proved to be an effective pain killer.

Laughter is a great beauty product. Have you ever noticed how attractive someone becomes after they laugh? Laughter stimulates circulation and gives us color while also toning up our face muscles and improving our expressions. We seem to sparkle.

Laughter provides a great face lift while lifting your spirit.

It is also very individual. It's part of our character. We will recognize a person's laugh. Some of us love a good belly laugh where it comes from deep down inside and rocks our whole body. Others may giggle like a tinkling bell. Still others may barely show amusement with twinkling eyes or slightly raised corners of the mouth. Some of us find humor in numerous aspects of life, while others find amusement to be a rare commodity.

How often do you have a good laugh?

This is a case where more is better. If you did not answer that you laugh several times a day, then it's time to build more laughter into your life. You might start a collection of jokes and cartoons that you find funny. Ask friends to share their favorite jokes. Watch funny movies. Sit at the mall or on a park bench and seek the humor in the scenes around you. Remember your own funny experiences and the funny incidents in which you were the central player. Laugh.

Remember that laughter is great medicine. Use it in large doses.

AgeEsteem is laughing often to feel and look healthier.

SEX

Beauty is the love of life that flows from the inside out.
It transcends age.

SEX. NOW THERE'S A WORD to catch your attention, no matter what your age.

It certainly had that affect on me at a dinner party we attended. Martin, a very debonair gentleman of 92, settled himself on the sofa, turned to me and said, "Sex! That is all they think about!"

Oh, yes. My attention was captured. I wanted to know more. Who were "they"? Before I could even ask, he continued. "See those lovely women across the room? I've known them for years. Now, because I'm a widower and single, they're constantly conniving to fix me up with some younger woman. Each time I see them they have someone new to present me to." And with twinkling eyes, he added, "I love it!"

I could easily understand the conspiracy. Here was a distinguished gentleman with a cane *à la* Maurice Chevalier, who was captivating. If the bounce was missing in his step, it was present in his eyes that conveyed a real passion for living.

Sex and age depend greatly on us if we want them to be exciting.

Sex is so much more than sexual intercourse. Just because we are past child bearing years does not mean that we do not want and enjoy sex. We do! In many ways it even becomes better. With maturity comes a different form of intimacy and concern for the other. It's a means of cherishing the present moment and all those special past moments all at the same time.

Sex is that feeling of wanting someone and feeling special at the same time. It's the intimacy of holding another close and feeling his or her warmth and breath. It's the comfort of knowing the other person intimately and accepting him as the person he is. It's the acceptance of who you are in your most natural state.

After more than forty years of marriage my heart still does flip flops if I am somewhere that I don't expect to see my husband and he walks into view. He still excites that special feeling.

Sex and age have something in common, besides the fact that they are both three letter words. They both depend greatly on us. If we want age to be exciting and intense, then we need to give it the same attention and effort. We need to give age that extra spice and passion just as we do sex.

A sexual relationship keeps us feeling young and nimble and truly alive. Part of being human is the desire to love and be loved. It's that feeling of warmth and sense of security that comes from being embraced in somebody's caring arms. Sex can be present or not.

The best relationships are those that develop naturally and allow you to get to know each other as individuals.

Don't be afraid of declaring your need for intimacy. Reach out to others. Several of my friends have used dating services to meet new friends and partners. It can be time intensive and emotionally wearing, but it can also be fun and result in new, lasting relationships. A natural means to meet others is to join activities, take lessons, play a sport or volunteer.

The best relationships are those that grow naturally and allow you to get to know each other as individuals. It builds as you discover common values and share activities and experiences. It's not because we are older that we need to feel rushed. Taking the time necessary to know each other will nurture a richer relationship. Let intimacy develop.

One of my favorite Snoopy cartoon cards is displayed on my dresser. The message says, "I think I need a hug." It reminds me that the best way to get a hug is to give a "hug"!

How will you bring intimacy into your life?

KEEP IT SAFE

Don't think that you are immune to HIV and AIDS infections because you are over 50. It is not true. It is essential that people of all ages practice safe sex.

There are startling statistics showing that HIV and AIDS infections are increasing among older people. In the US about 10 per cent of all new infections are in people older than 50 and a quarter of those are among men and women who are older than 60.

Age does not make us immune to HIV/Aids. Practice safe sex.

In many states there are programs to educate the older population on how to protect themselves. If this is not the case where you live, speak with your doctor. Those of us who are 60 and older grew up at a time when talk about sex was taboo. We didn't receive sex education. Even today you may not feel at ease talking about it. But seek information. Don't take any chances.

If you are sexually active, protect yourself. Practice safe sex.

AgeEsteem is acknowledging your need for
sexual intimacy and practicing safe sex.

JUST BE HAPPY

Past generations live through your smile; present generations return your smile; future generations will renew your smile.

WHEN OUR GODSON MARRIED IT offered the perfect occasion for my husband to share a few words of wisdom with the guests.

Most vivid were his closing remarks when he quoted a Chinese proverb that says, "If you want to be happy, just **be happy**." At first the guests smiled. It seemed like a joke. Then the real meaning sank in. What a simple statement! What a truth-filled message.

If I want to be happy, no matter what my age, it's up to me. If I want to be happy, then I should just be happy! I have the power to see the positive, the humor, the bright side of the experience, or I can dwell on the negatives and pain. The glass can be half full or half empty. We can not always control what happens to us as we journey through life, but we can decide how to react. It's our choice!

I have the power to see the positive, the humor and the bright side of the experience

Delbert, known as Deb, is now 93 years old and legally blind. When his wife of 60 years died several years ago, he could have decided to sit in a chair and feel sorry for himself, but that's not his style. Instead, he takes a daily ride on a stationary bike in the home where he lives, and finds numerous ways to keep up-to-date on current affairs, books, and new fads. His large print e-mails are uplifting and full of life and news. They provide a pleasant link to numerous friends and family. He wants to be happy, and he is!

Several years ago, he started mentioning June, the woman who read to him each day. She had now read to him for over 280 hours and had become a friend. His e-mails mentioned her more and more frequently. The hours that she read to him increased, as did references to her qualities. Then the signature on the e-mails became "Deb and June".

Finally an e-mail arrived saying that Deb and June had married.

When I visited them the following year, Deb explained how it happened. June used to join him in the evening after dinner to read to him, and then would walk back to where she lived in the farthest wing. One evening she started to laugh as she was leaving. Deb asked what was so amusing. June replied, "It just hit me that this is the first time in my life that I'm seeing someone regularly and walking home alone." From then on, Deb walked her back to her apartment. It was great exercise and he loved being gallant.

One day a specialist came to speak on personal financial planning. Deb had missed the group presentation, so he scheduled a private meeting with June accompanying him to read any papers. When they arrived and introduced themselves, with their separate last names, the financial counsellor said, "Oh, I see. I assume that you're planning to marry and want to arrange finances for the interests of your respective children."

As Deb tells the story, he then said to the financial advisor, "You, Sir, have realized what I've been slow to understand myself. Would you just give me a minute before we begin?" He then pulled out his handkerchief, placed it on the floor to kneel on, and taking the hand of June, asked her to be his wife. Apparently with no hesitation she said, "Yes!" and they proceeded with the meeting.

Happiness is contagious.

If you want to be happy, just be happy! Your happiness is contagious. It will draw people and opportunities to you. More happiness will follow.

How can you make today a happy day?

AgeEsteem is knowing that if you want to be happy, it is up to you.

CHAPTER 6

PERSONAL PURPOSE

Never base your decisions on another person's point of view.

Purpose is crucial to life at every age. It's the catalyst that prompts us to look forward to each new day with renewed energy. It is what gives us a reason to get up in the morning. Out of purpose grows our personal power.

The foundation of purpose and personal power is to understand that "I control my thinking and therefore my life."

I control my thoughts, and therefore my life.

Much is being done to combat the <u>external</u> effects of aging. Anti-aging creams, cosmetic surgery, bust-firmers, hair implants, sexual enhancement pills and weight patches are just a few of the products and techniques that we have available to us.

Thousands of books and reports have been written about the aging process. Many more have been written about how to stay young longer through exercise, diet, food supplements, laser treatments, massage, beauty applications and many products that will seemingly make you look and feel young. These are important aspects of dealing with growing older and wanting to retard the process. The problem is that this is "second hand."

THE MOST VITAL FACTOR

The most vital factor that influences aging is overlooked. This factor concerns my attitude. "How do I feel about myself? How good is my self-esteem in relation to aging? What is my attitude towards aging? How good is my AgeEsteem?" Having a positive internal view towards aging is absolutely critical if we are to age well.

> *My attitude offers me the key to aging happily,*
> *healthfully and with purpose.*

Our positive attitude is the key to living our age happily, healthfully and actively. This positive attitude is AgeEsteem. When we have strong AgeEsteem, we are able to make knowledgeable decisions. We exercise, eat healthfully and pamper ourselves because it is congruent with our inner image of ourselves.

If we decide to have cosmetic treatments to alter our appearance, it is our conscious decision to do so. We have not let ourselves be coerced by images convincing us we must pursue youth. We know that the treatment can only be successful if our AgeEsteem is strong. If I do not like myself before the treatment, I will not like myself after it is over. The treatment will only touch the surface. I will remain the same person within.

We are the age we feel ourselves to be.

We are the age we feel ourselves to be. Our inner attitude and our outlook towards life influence how we live. Our philosophy towards life marks us physically, emotionally, psychologically, intellectually and spiritually.

It is this personal goodwill towards ourselves through our AgeEsteem that allows us to take control, to identify who we are and to build a meaningful life at the age we are today.

A main ingredient of that meaningful life is summed up in one word, "purpose."

AgeEsteem is having a positive, happy attitude towards life that allows us to make decisions based on our own desires and needs.

THE POWER OF PURPOSE

Having a purpose enables us to step outside of
our own needs and problems, to focus on new opportunities
and to renew our energy as we take action.

ONE OF MY EARLY JOBS was directing a group of 40 volunteers, working in the geriatric ward of a psychiatric hospital. What I learned during that time could fill volumes. Each day was a day of discovery – discovery of new ideas, new approaches, and new experiences. Most important, though, was the revelation of untapped potential.

Our role as volunteers was to bring the outside world, the real world with its flaws and direct contact, into the ward. The philosophy of the director was that we would bring more to the patients by simply being ourselves, even though we were bound to make mistakes. At the same time, we were encouraged to experiment with new ideas and to introduce new activities.

When we have purpose it brings us personal power to do more!

What we learned was that having a purpose led to personal power.

Two anecdotes stand out in my mind.

The first happened when we decided to organize a dance. Only about half of the patients were independently mobile. They would be able to dance to their favorite tunes, while the others listened to the music and watched. It would definitely offer everyone a change of routine.

To our amazement, shortly after the music began, two people who could not walk got up to dance. The power of purpose! Yes, they were holding on to their partner – and they were dancing! They wanted to dance, so they did.

The second incident happened when I took a gentleman for a ride through the park. He had not walked for months, so I settled him into a wheelchair. After I had bumped him up one curb and then jolted him down another, he yelled, "Stop!" I stopped and asked him what was wrong. "You don't know how to wheel this chair properly." He then commanded in a booming voice, "You sit in it and let me show you how it is done." I helped him up. I then sat in the wheelchair and held my breath while he managed to get behind it and firmly take the handles. "This", he said, "is how it is done." He then proceeded to push me for the better part of a block before deciding that I had assimilated his teachings. The power of purpose!

Each of us needs to feel that we have purpose, that we have a reason to get up in the morning. We want to feel that we belong. This does not change with age. Perhaps it becomes more important. We each want to feel needed, to step outside ourselves, to relate to others in a meaningful way, and to subscribe to our world.

Every morning I get up thinking, "What can I do to make a difference?"

When my friend Paula sold her business, I asked her how she was adjusting to no longer being president of the company. She admitted that it was not an easy transition. When I asked what kept her going, she responded, "Every morning I get up thinking about where I can contribute. What can I do to make a difference?" What was once taken for granted must now be planned. Planning how to contribute enriches her life as she finds new ways to "make a difference."

Purpose turns us outward. It enables us to focus on others and to take action. Purpose prompts us to develop a new perspective, to step outside of ourselves and our problems, and to see the day as an opportunity.

As we begin to capture these opportunities, we find renewed energy and excitement. This brings better health and well-being which gives us the drive to do even more. It sparks an upward spiral of interest, contacts, actions and satisfaction.

AgeEsteem is living with purpose.

THE POWER OF BEING PRESENT

A great conversationalist knows how to listen.

WE DO NOT NEED TO manage a business or to move mountains to have a purpose. Sometimes it is enough just to be there for others. A favorite example is our friend Peter. Peter has multiple sclerosis and is confined to bed 90 percent of the time.

Peter is passionate about music, reads the daily paper for local news and remains informed on world issues via television. Since he is always accessible, welcoming and genuinely interested, friends of all ages seek him out. He is a spider in the middle of a web of relationships and valued information.

Most important, Peter actively listens with his heart as well as his ears and gives meaningful advice when it is sought. He is well aware of the important role he plays. Over the years he has learned that many of his visitors just need to be able to talk to someone. He offers them a non-judgemental ear while they work out their own solutions. Peter's presence is an important gift.

When you touch someone's life, you don't know what he will do with what you have given him. It does not matter. The joy is in the giving.

Opportunities surround us. They are like grapes. We just have to reach out and pluck them off the vine. Each of us has something special to offer.

AgeEsteem is being aware of our purpose
and finding opportunities to act on it.

REACHING OUT TO THE WORLD

As our world becomes smaller, my reach becomes greater.

As we acquire years, it is possible to stretch our talents to the wider community and the greater world. It may develop out of an opportunity to work with the local YWCA which has outreach to 124 countries, through elder hostel work travels, or from something you have designed or crafted which draws on your professional skills.

Go where there is no path; and leave a trail.

My husband, Gerard, participates in a team of retired technicians and engineers who have developed a water purifying system. The goal is to supply pure drinking water to areas where none is available. The accumulated professional expertise of these eight men amounts to 380 years. These volunteers have an amazing radius of influence. They raise funds and build relationships with organizations already providing programs within developing countries. They travel to designated sites to test the feasibility and then to work with the local people to build the system and train them to manage it. Presently they are installing water purifying systems in Cameroon and Kenya. This is their gift to the world.

There are many groups similar to this one working to improve our world. For example, my friend Mary just returned from China where she has spent three months teaching English. Another friend, Larry, participated in a building project with Habitat for Humanity.

When you light a lamp for someone else, it also brightens your own vision.

Would you like to share your talents to further benefit your neighborhood, country, or the world?

How would you like to share? You can begin today by investigating possibilities. You will find many opportunities by researching on the Internet. Service clubs, religious groups, governmental and non-governmental organizations, universities and senior groups also can be good sources of information.

Opportunities abound.

AgeEsteem is finding new challenges
and opportunities to reach out to the world.

CHAPTER 7
BUILDING SUPPORT

I was feeling lost…then you reached for my hand,
and I was home again.

W e all need other people around us some of the time, and many of us seek the company of others most of the time.

People are important to us for information, services, comfort, guidance, support and company. We learn from others and give to others. We also offer our assistance and share our know-how. Relationships are reciprocal.

Friendships are precious assets to our health and confidence.

Research studies emphasize a strong correlation between healthy aging and having regular contact with others. This is especially powerful when there is a common purpose shared. That purpose can encompass any common effort or ritual, such as helping to save Florida sea turtles, sharing religious traditions, playing bridge or golfing.

A danger with aging is to limit our social contacts. Many people have told me that they find it more difficult to make new friends each year. When I asked them how they built close friendships when they were younger, they answered that it usually revolved around a common interest or shared experience. They attended the same school, sang in the same glee club or had children who were the same age.

A key to AgeEsteem is to be active socially. Would you like to have more contact with others? Begin by participating in something that you enjoy. Why not take a class in auto mechanics or origami? You might volunteer at a children's museum, or get involved in politics. Plan an activity that motivates you and that will put you into contact with others.

You will become more confident as you nurture your emotional well-being by interacting with other people. It will also give you greater purpose in life, which also feeds your emotional and psychological health.

We are able to accomplish more when other people are there to assist us, guide us, encourage us and simply be there for us.

An important lesson that I have learned over the years is that it is essential to have a support team. This is true not only during difficult times. It's equally important when life goes smoothly. No one can do everything alone.

My dream to build a positive attitude towards aging is a prime example. I never could have done what I have without others supporting me in hundreds of different ways.

Today most people refer to their contacts as a network. A network is made up of professional and personal friends and acquaintances, people with whom we come into regular or occasional contact. We are able to accomplish so much more when other people are there to assist us, listen to us, advise us, guide us, encourage us, carry us, support us and simply be there for us. We need this at all stages of our lives.

I call this network my support system. Each person plays a role in my life and brings a special benefit to it. It doesn't matter whether it's a family member or friend, my hairdresser, minister, mail carrier, or a former colleague. All of them are part of my support system.

The people around us change as we move into new surroundings. It can be quite frightening. I know. When I was growing up we moved to a new state every four years. Then as an adult I married a man from Switzerland and moved to a foreign country with a language that I didn't understand. My husband was a tremendous help, but it was up to me to build friendships, become acquainted with a new dentist and doctor, civic leaders and neighbors. I had to constantly ask directions to find my way. It was overwhelming.

What amazes me as I look back is how rapidly I did adjust. I jumped into the language and culture with the goal to make them mine. Since I had to reach out to others for help, advice and guidance, I soon had a group of friends and acquaintances I could call by name. It was the beginning of my new support network.

There is no key to happiness. The door is always open.

My friend Martha had a similar experience when she moved into a retirement home. She was not at all certain that she wanted to be there. She did it for her children. "They worried about me living by myself, and the house really was too big for me." The problem was that she didn't know anyone in her new home and everything was unfamiliar. She felt lost during the first weeks. This changed, as she discovered the interesting opportunities to become actively involved.

Martha loved to tell stories. She had been called Mrs. Story Hour when she ran a children's program at the local library. Since she was still passionate about books and telling stories, she began giving book reviews in her new community. She met even more interesting people. Martha created a new network and continued to increase it because she reached out to others through her passion.

It's never too late. If your network does not yet exist, begin to create it today!

Become aware of the many people who touch your life, and people whose lives you influence in some way. Begin to make a list of the people you know. Maybe you already have a list you use for holiday cards or a club directory. Highlight the names of people you know. This is the beginning.

You will want to add family; friends; colleagues; service providers such as your hairdresser, doctor, dentist and delivery person; people from your place of worship, exercise and activity groups. The list is infinite. When you meet new people, add them to your list.

When I place someone new on my list, I like to indicate where we met and a few key words about them. This includes common interests, people, or dreams. I believe that all relationships are reciprocal. They are an exchange of interests, information, advice and services. They extend among all generations.

Goodness encourages goodness.

Your support network is made up of relationships, which means people with whom you give and take. The support is reciprocal. Do not keep score, though. It is a natural relationship. You will sometimes give more and sometime receive more.

Over the years, there have been multitudes of people who have reached out to me and helped me in some way. If I do not return their goodness directly, I nevertheless pass it on to someone else. Each time that I reach out to someone in need, I am not alone. All the people who helped me along the way are also reaching out through me. I continuously thank them by doing something for someone else. Goodness encourages goodness.

Be the first to reach out. Ask for help. Offer your assistance. Join a class to learn something or a book discussion group. Begin to widen your circle, one person at a time.

AgeEsteem is building social contacts
and feeling at ease to ask for help and to help others.

LIVING IN BALANCE

A balanced life brings harmony and peace.

BALANCE IS A NECESSARY INGREDIENT in life. Balance in our exercise routines. Balance in respect to time spent with family, work and social contacts. Balance in nature. Balance among sound, sight, touch, smell and taste. Balance is harmony.

Part of this harmony is having a balance of interaction among all ages. In preparing AgeEsteem® and this book, I brought together groups of people of all ages to explore their concerns about aging. I asked them, "What is essential to aging well, with satisfaction, health and dignity?"

A common response raised the importance of being in cross generational groups. It spoke to the need to have continued contacts with people of all ages. But it also went beyond that. People spoke about the need to have direct relationships and interaction with children, young adults and adults of all ages. It's an important ingredient of feeling that one belongs, is needed, and has a role in society.

Harmony represents a well-balanced approach to dealing with everyday happenings, both planned and unexpected.

Some seniors feel an advantage of age is the freedom to develop their own interests. Children have grown and moved elsewhere. Routines have changed. This frees up time for them to think of themselves.

Part of balance is to know how much time you need to be alone, and how much time you need with others. And to find a happy balance.

If you are dissatisfied with your life, ask yourself if this need for contact with other generations is being met in the dosage that is right for you. Balance is important.

AgeEsteem is seeking balance in all areas of your life.

THE IRISH PUB

No one said, "You're too old." or "You're too young."
They simply locked elbows and sang.

AN IRISH FRIEND, JOHN, and I have had many discussions around the topic of AgeEsteem.

We both feel strongly that older people give us a reference in life. They offer us a sense of stability and perspective no matter what is happening around us. They are a model for us.

John explained to me that as a young man he spent most evenings at the local pub. Pubs are an important part of the Irish culture. The community gathers in the local pub. It's where you go to see your friends.

"We always went to the pub where there were people of all ages," John explained. "We didn't just seek out young people. It was the mix of ages that drew us. I learned so much from the older people who were there. They had lived and knew what life was all about. Each day I learned from them."

Having a place where you can interact naturally
with people of all ages is important.

One concern with aging is loneliness. Spouses pass on. Friends and family move. Aging may bring physical difficulties that keep us from getting out and about easily and having contact with other people. The less we use the mobility that we do have, the more mobility we lose.

Having a place to find other people and to interact with all ages is important. This mixture of ages benefits each of us. It's natural. We learn from each other. We draw on the talents and interests of each other. The local Irish pub responds to this need. Without going far you can be among friends. We need to find a similar focus in our culture.

We can re-create the concept of an Irish pub in a different context. It may be found in the delight we have in taking our grandchildren or borrowed children to the circus, in a park visiting with friends, or in working out at a health club regularly. Many opportunities surround us. It's up to us to recognize them or to create them.

AgeEsteem is seeking contact with people of all ages
within a mix of generations.

READ MY HEART

When we focus on the hearts of those around us,
we discover the good, and the kind and the positive.

A WONDERFUL EXPRESSION HAS BECOME part of our family. It's "Read my heart!"

When my father was dying, his tongue was so badly swollen, that it was impossible for him to be understood when he spoke. It was up to me to translate what I thought he wanted to express. I gave up trying to read his lips. I decided that the only approach left to me was to read his heart.

During recent visits we'd had numerous conversations about life and what was important to each of us. I anticipated his words would be coming straight from his heart. We both knew that the people he was seeing then would probably not have another opportunity to hear what he wanted to say.

When a nurse was extremely gentle and caring, Dad moved his mouth and I translated, "Thank you for your gentle care." The last time his doctor visited him, Dad tried to speak. Again I read his heart and interpreted, saying, "I love you." I'm convinced it was the message he wanted to convey to this doctor who'd always been honest in his messages, yet caring. It was relatively easy to read Dad's heart because he'd openly shared what he wanted to say when he wanted to say it throughout life.

How many of us haven't done this, and still have words to share? Now is the opportunity to say: "I appreciate your loving words, kind gestures, encouragement and confidence in my efforts…"

When we focus on the heart of a person, we begin to learn who she really is and to relate at a deeper level.

It's uplifting to focus on the hearts of those around us, because we start to see the good, the kind and the positive. We look beyond the facade of the person to find the real concerns and preoccupations. It allows us to go beneath the externally visible and discover the real person within. It helps us to relate at a deeper level.

Read my heart and you'll find messages of happiness and encouragement. You'll read, "I love you." "Thank you for being there for me." "It means a lot to me when you greet me by name." "I enjoy your notes." "Thank you for teaching me how to use the Internet." "Your phone call made my day." "Remembering our time together warms my thoughts." "Your smile lights my world." "I'm proud of you!" "You are beautiful, inside and out!" "Your energy is contagious."

Yes. Read my heart!

Whose heart will you read today?

AgeEsteem is reading the hearts of those around us.

SAY IT NOW

Never put off telling someone what is on your heart today.

ISN'T IT WONDERFUL TO KNOW that others care, that you are appreciated, and that someone is better because of something you did? It's encouraging to be praised for what you do well. You are also more apt to do it again.

Sometimes we seem to be bashful about complimenting or praising others. How sad it is when we lose track of people or they die and we have not yet told them what they mean to us.

When I was 16 and camping in Yosemite Park with my family, I spent an afternoon with a graduate student working as a forest ranger for the summer. He cared about what I thought and what I believed. In that short afternoon my values and dreams were confirmed. He instilled in me the belief that I could realize my dreams. Now, almost 50 years later I look on him as one of those special people who left a lasting imprint. I wish I could thank him.

Today, I try to express my thanks and appreciation to people often. It's important to share praise and words of encouragement now. Who knows when we will get another chance to put into words what we want others to know?

Those who have influenced our lives
continue to live through our actions.

Hattie, who was my parents' generation, was a mentor and a guiding light for me at a time when I was making life decisions as a young adult. She remained a special friend. One day I received a telephone call to say that Hattie had died. The family asked my permission to include in the bulletin a message I had written to Hattie eight years earlier. She had kept it in her night table and regularly asked people to read it to her.

It read, "You have been – and continue to be – such a special role model and influence in my life, Hattie. I will always be sharing a touch of you each time I reach out to help someone else. I know there are hundreds who will be doing the same. Thank you for all you have given me. I love you, Bonnie."

Let people know what they mean to you and what you most admire in them. Thank them for their gifts of friendship, guidance and support. There is no time like the present. Say it now.

Who are the people who are important in your life? This may include your family, friends, barber or hairdresser, nurse or doctor. It may be the person you meet regularly on the bus. List these people who are special to you.

Next to their name indicate why they are special in your life. It may be one particular trait that you like about them. You may want to refer to a specific incident that touched you. Whatever it is, write it next to their name now.

An example is Mike, who delivers the mail, because he whistles as he comes up the walk and always calls out a cheery "hello".

Now, select five of these people to thank. How would you like to tell each of them what you appreciate about them?

Taking Mike as an example, tomorrow when you hear him whistling you might call out to him saying that you would like to tell him something. When he approaches say, "Thank you for your cheerful greeting, Mike. I look forward to hearing you whistling and to your greeting each day." You could also put a special note for him on the mailbox. You might buy him a tee shirt saying, "Whistle While You Work." A bag of homemade cookies with a message is another idea.

It doesn't really matter how you tell the person. Use your imagination and have fun. Mike probably has no idea how much his cheery hello means to you.

Set yourself a goal to thank two people each week. As you continue this exercise, you will probably find that your list grows. And it becomes easier to express your appreciation.

You are a powerful role model in your angry moments
as well as the joyous ones.

What about the other words you have in your heart? The words, "I'm sorry." or "Forgive me." or "I miss you." Now is the time to express those words freely, too.

Share what is in your heart with others. They say that people do not remember what your title was or your golf handicap. What they do remember is how you made them feel.

You are beginning a positive new approach to saying what matters.

Continue to say it now!

AgeEsteem is feeling confident to recognize the good in others and to praise them. It is also being strong enough to say you are sorry.

CHAPTER 8

SPIRITUALITY

EMBRACE YOUR SPIRITUALITY

Explore your inner voice. Listen to your spiritual soul.

Wwhat is spirituality?

If we look at the definition of spiritual in <u>Collins English Dictionary</u> we find, "relating to a person's beliefs as opposed to his or her physical or material needs."

Spirituality brings an inherent understanding of
how everything comes together in a meaningful way.

In my professional experience working with people to define what motivates them, it is evident that spirituality is often a strong factor and that it carries multiple definitions. For some spirituality relates to religion and their belief in a greater power. Other personal definitions include an inner sense of how everything comes together; a sense of balance and justice; a belief in some greater force; a deep perception and natural understanding

107

that cannot necessarily be put into words but that brings a feeling of peace and harmony with what surrounds us such as nature, people and animals; a communication with nature and the natural relationships that tie our world together; a guiding light. It is an inherent understanding that everything comes together in a meaningful way.

Stop here for a minute to think about your own life. How do you define spirituality? How important is spirituality in your life? Can you define some specific examples?

Spirituality embraces values, morals and a meaning of life. People who feel a meaning and purpose for life feel happier and more satisfied in their lives. Spirituality is related to better mental and physical health.

Spirituality weaves throughout all aspects of life. It sets people apart. It gives them a deeper comprehension and reduces barriers and discrimination or bias.

Spirituality weaves throughout all aspects of your life.

My maternal grandmother, Jenny Elvira Blewfield, was a tiny little woman with beautiful translucent skin with a slight pinkish tint that made her look healthy and happy at all times. She was a woman who laughed, loved and truly lived each day no matter how difficult present circumstances might seem. In her memoirs, Living the Years, there is a passage I treasure.

It reads, "…ours was an inheritance worth much to us and we, in turn, have passed it on to our children. Our list includes practical common sense, courage in facing every-day living with faith, hope and zest, making do with little and enjoying sharing with others of our money, time and special talents."

I love this quote for two reasons. First because it is an excellent recipe for living life with meaning and joy; and secondly because the underlying thread among all that she mentions is, I believe, spirituality. Yet, it is explained in practical terms. Spirituality is the non-material. It is the practical common sense that comes through the experience of living and learning. It is courage to face each new day with faith, hope and zest. It is to believe in the future and to live fully in the present. And, yes, it is also the joy of living by being and doing and sharing what you have with others through your time, money and special talents.

Maybe you are a very spiritual person and naturally tune into what I am saying. Perhaps you are spiritual but have never felt inclined to develop it. You may also be someone for whom spirituality is a foreign word with no personal meaning. We are all different. What is important here is to recognize that spirituality does play an important role in our lives. It is up to you to decide whether you wish to develop your own spirituality further.

Transcend your environment and become one with it.

I have an old fashioned hammock which hangs between two majestic centennial trees. It is my refuge, the special place that I return to in the late afternoon to decompress and listen to my inner self as I bask in nature. I have no special plan. Between those two sentinels I connect with history and traditions of the past as well as my visions for the future, while being fully in the present. I find peace for my soul to yawn, stretch and renew itself. Gratitude for the beauty and balance of God's world fills me. I know that I am not even a tiny speck within this tremendous universe; yet I am important in my finite role within the greater plan.

People ask if it is possible to develop a sense of spirituality. I believe you can. If you would like to try, I encourage you to start with one of the following exercises to touch down with your inner self.

* Walk in the rain. Stroll. Don't race. Enjoy the fresh air. It actually smells and even tastes different in the rain. Get wet. Let the drops fall on your face. Feel the moment. Concentrate on this one moment in time. Let your thoughts stray. Lean into your thoughts and follow them.

* Keep a journal of your thoughts and feelings. Do not plan what you will write. Just let the words flow. This is a powerful way to listen to yourself and really hear what is going on inside your mind.

* Sit in a park, yard or field. Be quiet and tune into what goes on around you. Notice the movement of insects and birds. Feel the breeze and the difference of the sun's heat as clouds float by. Listen to the sounds of nature. Breathe in the fresh air. Smell the multiple fragrances surrounding you. Open your mouth

and breathe deeply. Taste the flavors of your surroundings. Close your eyes. Transcend your environment and become one with it. Enjoy.

AgeEsteem is knowing that however insignificant it may seem, you have a role within the greater plan of the universe.

POSITIVE ATTRACTION

As I throw my thoughts out to the universe,
magic seems to happen – they become reality.

IN CHINESE FOLKLORE THERE IS a saying that when a child is born, his spirit is connected by an invisible red thread to all of the people who will become important to that child. As the child grows older, the threads shorten and become tighter, bringing these people closer to him. The thread draws their destinies together.

Whether or not you believe in predestination, this is an interesting concept. I have often felt in life that I was drawn to specific people at particular moments in time. My husband of over 40 years is an example. Had I met him a few weeks earlier or a few weeks later, or in different circumstances would I have been attracted to him or him to me? Looking back it seems to me that magic was at work to make it happen.

Today people continue to pop into my life from unexpected places at a moment when our paths are meant to merge. The timing is perspicacious. Magic continues to work for me as I throw my vision out to the universe.

Positive attraction is, I believe, strongly related to spirituality. Perhaps you have experienced this power yourself. Some call it the self fulfilling prophecy. We think about something and it actually happens. It becomes reality. Our thoughts create our future.

Worry is emotional and drains energy.
Concern is intellectual and helps us find solutions.

The power of the mind is tremendous, overwhelmingly powerful at times. This is why it is so important to keep our thoughts focused on the good and the positive. When we think about something we draw it to us. Our thoughts are magnetized to attract action to them.

I once asked my father if he had worried about us as we four girls were growing up. His response was inspiring, though simple. He explained that he had not worried about us, because worry is emotional. It focuses on anxiety and unease over what might happen and nourishes negative thoughts.

Instead of worrying he said that he was concerned. To be concerned is to be interested and involved. It is intellectual and focuses on positive outcomes. Focusing on positive outcomes attracts them to us.

Our thoughts create our future.

Being interested and involved and focused in our thoughts on what we want life to be draws that life to us. Learning to think positively was a way of life in our family. Before leaving for camp one summer I remember wondering out loud to my mother if I would have a good time at camp. Her response became cemented into my thinking. She said, "If you decide that you'll have a good time, you will; so why not make up your mind now?" She was right. I had a wonderful time.

Even today when I have trepidations about something in the future, I simply decide in my mind how I want it to be. I am very rarely disappointed. Usually it is better than I had pictured.

As a child I naturally looked eagerly towards what I would do next. As an adult I began to consciously look forward to each new event and occasion. I did not always know what I wanted as I went into a new experience, but I did know it would be positive.

It is the same today. People tell me that I am lucky to have so many opportunities to contribute my talents in unique ways, to speak in front of interesting audiences, to meet exceptional people and to have so much energy. They are right. I am lucky. But much of that luck grows out of my spiritual belief in the good and positive and in looking forward to each new day with optimism. Once you get started, it becomes a never ending upward spiral.

An effective exercise to get you started building your own upward spiral is something I repeat every four to six months. You might want to try this.

Visualize beyond what you wish to attain.

In your notebook make a wish list. Without stopping to think, write down as many wishes or desires that come to mind. Nothing is too wild, silly or impossible. Let them flow directly from your head to your pen. Keep writing rapidly without analyzing what you write. When you have filled at least two pages with your wishes, read them.

Are you surprised at what you wrote? I am usually amazed at many of mine. Many of them seem unrealistic and removed from what I am doing today – but not from what I want to be doing tomorrow!

Put this list aside. Two months later, look at it again. If you are like me, you will find that several of these wishes have already become reality. We attract to us what we think about. Writing these wishes down on paper helped to lock them into our subconscious which has been hard at work during these past months.

AgeEsteem is focusing our thoughts on the positives of today and picturing what we wish our life to be like in the future.

REJOICE!

Give thanks for this day, and treat it like a gift.

DO YOU EVER FEEL DOWN in the dumps questioning why everything goes wrong in your life? Do you find yourself commiserating with yourself over your bad fortune?

Granted, we all have moments when we find ourselves being sucked into a whirlpool of negativism, seemingly out of control. We do not even realize that we are the ones who increase the speed as we race down into the pit of despair. It is as though we are falling, falling, falling.

Some of you will rapidly admit that you have experienced this, or are even on the edge of the whirlpool now. Others may have to go on a memory search to remember the moments when this has happened.

The good news is that there is a cure! Next time you feel that the world has walked out and forgotten you, rejoice! Give thanks.

Does this sound crazy? It is not crazy at all. It is very effective.

When you feel like the world has forgotten you, rejoice!

Psychologists tell us that in order to reverse our mindset; we need a symbolic splash of cold water, something to shake us up so that we break our present thought pattern.

Can you remember a time when you were lying on a beach and someone splashed a pail of cold water on your warm skin? The shock of the unexpected cold water interrupted your thoughts. You forgot whatever you had been thinking about just before the splash of cold water. Your mind switched immediately to the cold, unexpected shower.

Instead of jumping into a cold shower the next time your thoughts start rolling downhill, rejoice. Look at what you have to be grateful for.

Begin with one event or capability that is positive in your life. Look at yourself as though you were your best friend. How would you praise yourself? Many of us find this difficult at first. Although we may compliment others, most of us are not in the habit of praising ourselves.

Write that one positive attribute on a sheet of paper. Post it where you will see it regularly such as on the refrigerator or a mirror.

Each time you look at it say, "I am thankful that…"

Add to this list regularly. Think of the people, situations and events in your life that are positive. Throw out any negative thoughts that sneak in. They are no longer worth your time. Seek out the positive in your life.

Seek out the positive in the people around you.

Anticipate the positives in the future.

What will amaze you as you use this technique is that it will not only change your thinking day by day; it will also turn your life onto new positive paths.

Try it. You have nothing to lose. It does not even cost money. In fact, it can economize funds for you as you become healthier and more constructively active.

This is especially important for us as we grow older. We need to recognize that we may have some physical limits with age. Perhaps we now walk rather than run. But there are always reasons to rejoice.

Greet each day as a gift.

Shirley was diagnosed with macular degeneration during her 50's and soon was unable to see to read or drive. She recognized friends by voice and body outline. Despite her eyes, she gave writing and speaking workshops. She wrote seven books after the age of 60. Most people had no idea that her sight was seriously impaired. Break of day was Shirley's favorite moment because she could fully enjoy the colors. She lived in Florida where year round she swam in the pool at dawn. She began her day rejoicing in the splendor of the rainbow of colors in the lightening sky.

When Jim died several neighbors were curious about a habit he had of talking to the sky each morning. They asked if it was some special ritual. I smiled at their question. Jim had explained this ritual to me. "When I wake in the morning it's always somewhat of a surprise to see that I'm still here. Each day is a gift." He went on to explain that once he was dressed, he would step outside to greet the day by looking at the sky and saying, "This is the day which the Lord hath made. Let us rejoice and be glad in it."

Both Shirley and Jim were people who enjoyed life and had energy to make a positive difference in the lives of others. I believe that a major factor in this was their gratitude for the wonders of the day and the realization that each day is a gift. They did not have time to find negatives. They were too busy rejoicing!

Smile to yourself before you go to sleep. It warms your dreams.

AgeEsteem is rejoicing in the blessings of each day.

CHAPTER 9

MY LASTING LEGACY

THE MANDATE

We grow up in one world and we become adult in another.

each generation has its mandate.

My mother-in-law was an amazing woman who ruled her world right up to the moment she left us at age 96. She was a woman of her times, strong as steel but with a heart as large as the Rocky Mountains. While studying at the University of Geneva in the early thirties as one of a handful of women, she crossed the Atlantic to study for a semester at Temple University in Philadelphia. She often commented to me that she grew up as part of the interim generation. Born in 1908, she was part of the generation that began the movement of equality and liberty for women in Switzerland but enjoyed few rights themselves.

We stand of the shoulders of those who go before us.

She explained that her generation was the interim generation because they grew up in one world and became adult in another. She was a child at a time when children were to be seen and not heard; yet her children and grandchildren were encouraged to speak up and speak out. Women in her generation did not work outside the home unless it was of utmost necessity; yet her daughters-in-law found this to be an interesting dimension in their lives. Although it was the women of her generation who fought for women's suffrage, rare were those who eventually held political office.

At the same time, the men of her generation carried the burden of being a successful provider for the family's needs, while their sons often shared this role with their wives who worked outside the home. Men of the interim generation were neither expected to change diapers nor to have direct daily contact with their children. Discipline was their main parental role; yet many of their sons bathed and fed their little ones with pleasure.

This amazing woman, along with others of her generation, paved the way for those of us who have followed, making our journey one of greater choices and opportunities for both genders.

Each generation contributes towards the next.

Each generation evolves, sometimes imperceptibly, as it prepares the way for the next.

Each generation has its own mandate to shape and form our world. It is the root of progress. My generation that grew out of the Second World War is no different.

For the first time in recorded history, seniors are tipping the demographic balance with the population of people aged 55 and older representing an extraordinary proportion. Soon this will become the largest segment of society in percentage of the population.

We are in the privileged position to be aware of this and to be able to prepare for it. Much is being done through advocacy and health and nutrition. More must be done.

The greatest need, however, is for us, the seniors of today and tomorrow, to put a new spin on our own attitudes toward aging. It is up to us to grow a new positive attitude within ourselves and society. We must define what age and aging should represent today. We have the strength in numbers and in experience to make a difference. It is for us, the people of senior generations, to lead society into this new paradigm.

This begins with each of us feeling good about ourself. We must have AgeEsteem, self-esteem that includes a positive relationship with our chronological age. With AgeEsteem, we will have the power to lead our society into a healthier future.

I once heard a speaker insist, "If you want to change the world, you must begin with the block you live on." It's clear. If I want to grow a positive attitude towards aging, then I must begin with myself. Only then can I reach out to those around me. I need to feel so good about my age that I become contagious so others begin to catch the AgeEsteem bug and positively infect other neighborhoods and beyond.

Think of yourself as a role model for others as you practice the concepts within these pages. Become an AgeEsteem® ambassador. Use and assimilate the secrets shared here and attract others to you. We all want to emulate people who have an inner glow of confidence and well being. Think of the times that you have gravitated towards someone you did not know because their positive vibes drew you to them. You thought, "I'd like to meet that person." Or perhaps you even said to yourself, "I'd like to be like her."

There is a magnetic power that attracts us to people who feel good about themselves. These are people who feel secure within themselves and show genuine interest in others. Age is no factor.

Let your AgeEsteem show. Become a model for others.

AgeEsteem is becoming an AgeEsteem® role model for others.

FROM PIMPLES TO PERSPECTIVE

We move from pimples and uncertainty
to maturity and new opportunities.

TWO MATURE WOMEN ARE DISCUSSING their aches and pains while reminiscing about the joys of being young.   A third woman who overhears their conversation strides over to them and says, "You mean you would prefer pimples and acne, wondering if you will ever be noticed by the opposite sex, searching for your own identity, and being on an all time high one minute and at rock bottom the next?"

I love this illustration. We have moved from pimples and uncertainty to maturity and an opportunity to launch our lives in new directions using the perspective that we have gained. We no longer need to search for our identity. We know who we are and can use that knowledge to make our lives more meaningful and purposeful.

Perspective provides us with wisdom to plan our future.

For your life to be meaningful, you must define what that word represents for you. What could you do now to make your life fulfilling for you? Would this include travel, working in the slums of your city, volunteering at the local museum, building a closer relationship with your children and grandchildren, learning a new skill or teaching one? Answers are endless and depend on you.

It is important to recognize what the word "meaningful" means to you for your life. Equally important is to decide how to build that meaning into your life. When we have AgeEsteem we recognize what we have learned through the experience of living. Hardships and joyous celebrations of learning, growing and sharing have propelled us to today. We are able to plan and anticipate how we want to utilize this experience.

With each year we gain valuable knowledge, experience and understanding. The world needs our maturity and wisdom.

Wisdom

* Brings a deeper understanding of people and relationships.
* Gives us perspective to see things in relation to values as well as needs.
* Enables us to set priorities and solve problems based on a comprehension of the bigger picture.
* Represents accumulated knowledge and learning.
* Empowers us to use our experience and knowledge to make sensible decisions.

How do you define the word "meaningful" for your life?

AgeEsteem is valuing our own maturity and wisdom.

MY LEGACY OF WISDOM

Being able to use the past with its experience of living
is a gift I have to share.

SO MUCH OF WHAT WE learn does not come from formal lessons or books. It is gained through the experience of living. These living experiences include relationships, travel, work, meeting people, and the process of maturing, and testing and fine-tuning what we learn.

An organization which I am proud to be part of is Legacy® Memory Bank. Legacy's mission is to inspire future and current generations to build on the experience, wisdom and values of today's leaders in all areas of humanity. Legacy recognizes the importance of capturing the essence of how these leaders became who they are today. What molded them and who inspired them? What key incidents influenced their lives? Their story is an important legacy.

We are the living echoes of those who have taught us
through word and example.

You, too, have a story to tell. I would like to encourage you to think about your own legacy. What would you like your grandchildren and future generations to know about you? I suggest that you share your legacy in two ways.

1. Write your memoirs. You might research special workshops or classes on writing your memoirs or autobiography. There are many books available in which you can record your memoirs, some of which have questions to inspire you. The Internet is another good source for information, forms and classes. You might also make an audio or audiovisual recording.

2. Write your Legacy of Life's Lessons. The following pages will guide you.

As a teacher, trainer and coach, I know that the best way to truly assimilate what you learn is to teach it to someone else. When you share information or a new technique by explaining it or showing the process to someone else so that they understand, you cement the knowledge in your mind.

It is no wonder that you and I have so much to share. We have experienced and re-experienced many lessons. We have also taught others on a daily basis in a multitude of ways for decades, and have assimilated our lessons well.

LEGACY OF LIFE'S LESSONS

What are some of the lessons that life has taught you?

Put these lessons into words. Take a few minutes to think about what you have learned that you could not have learned in a text book or on the

Internet. These will be lessons that you have learned through experience. They are the result of trial and error, of relationships, travels, work and mental and physical efforts.

Many valuable lessons are learned through experience.

An example might be, "Life has taught me to listen to my gut when I meet someone new. It tends to be right 90% of the time."

Make a list of these lessons. Write as many as possible. Begin with "Life has taught me…"

Once you have listed these lessons, go back to read them. The life lessons that you have listed are precious gifts to be shared. They represent wisdom that you have acquired and are now able to pass on to others. Although we may offer our wisdom regularly, we rarely think of it as that. Nor do we gage the full importance of what we can offer.

When you begin to think about what your Legacy of Life's Lessons actually represents, you will realize what great value it carries. That is why I encourage you to define this legacy of lessons more finely.

Refer to your list of Lessons of My Life that you have completed. Rephrase each lesson into a sentence of advice to share with others.

Refer to the previous example, "Life has taught me to listen to my gut when I meet someone new. It tends to be right 90% of the time."

We might rephrase it to read, "When you meet someone for the first time, tune in to what your inner instincts tell you. Listen with your whole being."

What a rich heritage this represents! You will want to share this written legacy with others. How do you plan to do this?

Ideas from AgeEsteem® workshop participants who have written their Legacy of Life's Lessons include: writing a lesson on a note card when writing to friends; making a book of lessons to give as a present; writing a "Wisdom Will" to document for posterity the most important things you learned in this lifetime, how you learned them, how you practiced them, those that you mastered and those that remain a challenge.

Now it is up to you!

AgeEsteem is sharing our legacy of lessons gained through living.

NOW IT IS UP TO YOU!

THE CONCEPTS AND TECHNIQUES IN these pages are now yours. I challenge you to perfect them. Continue to stretch and grow. Aging is wonderful. To age is to live.

Be alive with AgeEsteem.

As more of us gain personal AgeEsteem, the attitude of society will change. AgeEsteem will become the norm, and you and I will be seen as important contributing members of society.

I am interested in hearing how you use these concepts. How do you relate them to your life? Which one called out to you most loudly? How are you practicing it?

Visit www.AgeEsteem.com and share your story and questions with me. I look forward to hearing from you.

FAVORITE RESOURCES

www.AgeEsteem.com

Tips, stories and newsletter for people wanting to live their age fully

http://www.bumc.bu.edu/Dept/Content.aspx?DepartmentID=361&
pageID=5741

Boston University School of Medicine with a wealth of information and links

http://www.census.gov/compendia/statab/brief.html

U.S. Census Bureau

http://www.Census.Gov/ipc/www/idbsum.html

World Summary Demographic Data

www.GlobalAging.org

Focus on needs and potential within global economy

Includes links to other sites with valuable information on aging

www.Implicit.Harvard.edu/implicit/

Implicit Association Test (Demonstration & Research)

www.LegacyMemoryBank.org

In-depth audiovisual interviews of people who shape the world in all areas of humanity to inspire future generations

www.RealAge.com

Tips and tests to healthy aging

www.worldywca.org

Information on global issues where women of all ages are striving to make a difference

BIOGRAPHY

BONNIE LOU FATIO (FA SEE O)

"AgeEsteem is the fruit of 64 years of living, learning and embracing life. It has grown out of years of working with motivational issues and coaching people with diverse needs and backgrounds. Everything I share has been not only used, tested and refined. It is also who I am. If I can do it, so can you." —BONNIE LOU FATIO

BONNIE LOU FATIO, Founder of **AgeEsteem®,** is an internationally recognized motivational speaker who inspires and challenges. In her sixties, she feels that life becomes more exciting each day! For the last twenty years she has specialized in motivation and its power to influence positive change in individuals and organizations.

Born the second of four daughters, Bonnie's personal story is often viewed as a fairytale. She grew up in Methodist parsonages in the Midwest. Her first job was babysitting with a neighbor's children at age ten, which made it possible for her to purchase her first bicycle. It was a time when a change of clothing, one good pair of shoes and a bath on Saturday night was the norm. Healthy food and laughter were supplemented with love, strong values and a positive view of life.

Bonnie worked to pay her studies at Michigan State University where she earned a BA in Special Education. Practical experience in these multiple jobs, which extended from telephone operator to waitress to model, provided a rich understanding of 'the real world'.

During Bonnie's junior year she met her future Swiss husband, married two years later and moved to Geneva, Switzerland. Opportunities have abounded during the forty years that have followed: jobs in education, business and healthcare; board memberships ranging from IT start-up to home for the aged; being elected to the Geneva City Council; leading an organization of 1'400 women; committing professional time to several international organizations; promoting women; and starting her own successful company, BLEWFIELD ASSOCIATES *Energizing individuals - Enriching organizations*, which specializes in motivation and helping people shine through their special talents and interests in their work and in their private lives.

Bonnie's vision for **AgeEsteem,** is a world where age and aging are celebrated and people of all ages are respected as contributing members of society. For this to happen each of us needs to feel good about ourselves at the age we are today, every day.

AgeEsteem is a natural offspring of Bonnie's private life experiences and professional career. Throughout her career, Bonnie has been involved in issues relating to older people. She has directed a team of 40 volunteers in a geriatric hospital, and served on the boards of several retirement homes. She has worked with groups and coached individuals approaching retirement, and conducted substantial primary research on what people see as the challenges and solutions to having personal esteem as they age.

Community Leadership is an important dimension of Bonnie's life. She has held leadership roles in the World YWCA, as Vice President of the Career Women's Forum where she led the Women on Boards initiative, and also with other local leaders to support the United Nations High Commissioner for Refugees. She is a member of the Board of Legacy.

EDUCATION

She has a Bachelor of Arts degree in Special Education plus a Teachers Certificate from Michigan State University, U.S.A. and a Master of Arts degree in Human Resources Development with honors from Webster University in Geneva, Switzerland.

PERSONAL

Family and friends are treasured. Bonnie and her husband, Gérard Fatio, have a daughter Laetitia, son-in-law Christophe, and granddaughter, Jessica, born June 2, 2007. Bonnie's happiest moments are when family and friends surround the table and conversations and laughter abound.

Bonnie is invited regularly to speak about AgeEsteem in the US and Europe. She has traveled to meet with people, learn, train, lead groups and speak publicly in multiple countries outside of the U.S. and Europe including Australia, Bangladesh, China, Japan, Kenya, Philippines, S. Korea, and Uganda.

AGEESTEEM SUPPORTERS AND DOUBT BUSTERS

Suzanne Hough

Debby Phelps

Rich Phelps

Christophe Gaillard

Simona Ferrar

June Jolley

Doris Pagelkof

George Slaughter

Carol Spinner

Valsa Verghese

Jill Allan

Lynn Adams

Don Adams

Cary Adams

Nane Annan

Peter Baker

Jennifer Baur

Rev. John Beach

Stephen Beekman

Jane Bennett

Solange Bermens

Cindy Bernat

Evie Breakstone

Isabelle Buholzer

Valerie Buxton

Laura Cantini

Joanne Cardinal

Thierry Ceillier

Roy Chacko

Elizabeth Chapin

Betty Clark

Peter Cloutier

Richard Cole

Jody Colvard

Elizabeth Cook

Barb Crowfoot

Maria Anna Di
Marino

Helen Drew

Clark Elliott

Gina Empson

Kristin Engvig

Beatrice Etienne

Victoria Feldstein

Inma Fernandez

Judy Filusch

Wolf Filusch

Leslie Finn

Gladys Foster

Ann Gaillard

Xavier Gaillard

Judith Gerhart

Jennifer Giunta

Hausler

Catherine Graf-Stern	Caroline Miller	David R. Reed
Pamela Grant	H.E. Phumzile	Charles Revkin
Constance J. Grote	Mlambo-Ngcuka	Linda Revkin
Denis Grote	Beatrice Meier Moesli	Eliane Rey
Jamie Harmon	Ann Moffett	Linda Richards
Ann Hornung-Soukup	Linda Moore	Genie Ritthaler
Beth Houston Teja	Shawn Moore	Suzanne Rumphorst
Robert Huck	Pascale Morand	Ann Rutledge
Ania Jakubowski	Reem Najjar	Karen Saddler
Lisa Jimney	Luciana Niven	Ambassador Konji
Ron Johnson	Julia O'Connor	Sebati
Dr. Ann Kato	Susanne Paul	Alex Stauffer
Patricia Kicak	Doris Penning	Jean-Pierre Stauffer
Christopher Koch	Fritz Penning	Doug Stevenson
Hardy Korver	Helen Penton	Kristi J. Stingley
Yogi Krejan	Vernon Penton	Dorothy Stockell
Gisele Lalibeté	Lois Perry	Charles Strommer
Joy Lawrance	Ron Perry	Felicity Strommer
Lois Lawson	Lynn Pierce	Carol Swanson
Karen Lewis	Nicolas Porter	Alexandra Taylor
Laurence Levrat	Bob Posey	Krizia de Verdier
Sabine Lufkin	Karen Prudente	Penny Vincent
Anna Masson	Robert Race	Brigitte Vought
Michael McKay	Danièle Ramenen	Pam Walsh
Lorna Michaelson	Andrea Rechsteiner	Sheila Walsky

Pat Warman

Virginia Williams

Dorna Wilson

Karen Wilson

Lucia Wolf

Jane Lee Wolfe

Alexandra Woog

Raoul Wuergler

Monica Zetzsche

Dr. Dominique de Ziegler

Carol Zundel

Daniel Zundel

MEMBERS, COLLEAGUES AND FRIENDS OF

Blewfield Associates

World YWCA

Legacy® Memory Bank

Career Women's Forum

Global Action for Aging

Global Women in International Trade

American International Women's Club of Geneva

American International Club of Geneva

Business and Professional Women

European Professional Women's Network

W.I.N.

Performance Development Partners

ECLOF

Muenker Media

International Corporate Services

Global Financial Literacy

FunMoneyGood Network

Women in Podcasting

The Blewfield Cousins

BONUS

SIGN UP TODAY
FOR YOUR FREE MONTHLY
AGEESTEEM® E-ZINE

"AGING WITH PIZZAZZ!©"

IN *"AGING WITH PIZZAZZ! ©"* Bonnie Lou Fatio shares monthly tips and techniques illustrated with real life vignettes and humor as she challenges you and guides you to age with pizzazz.

- Recognize, support and celebrate the person you are – at the age you are today, everyday..

- Discover the value of age as an important dimension of your personal esteem.

- Build positive thoughts and attitudes toward age.

- Live in the present. – Build a meaningful future.

- Enjoy Ageesteem .

Pizzazz represents liveliness, animation, vivacity, sprightliness, life, verve, energy. It stands for power, vigor, vitality, drive, potentiality, strength, authority. It also refers to enterprise, initiative, and spunk. All of these are pieces of AgeEsteem.

Sign up for your FREE *"AGING WITH PIZZAZZ!*©*"* NOW.

Go to <u>www.AgeEsteem.com</u> and sign up for your free
E-Zine/Newsletter.

A PASSIONATE COMMITMENT

A PERCENTAGE OF MY ROYALTIES from this book will be donated directly to the World YWCA Global Fund which provides training to women of **all** ages, also benefiting children and men.

My passionate commitment has led me to annually contribute finances and a month of my professional time to the YWCA during the past five years. I have personally witnessed in several countries the effectiveness of YWCA programs ranging from adult literacy, basic hygene and managing micro-credit, to child and eldercare, HIV/Aids prevention, and governance.

Founded in 1855, the YWCA today reaches more than 25 million women and girls in 125 countries, providing them with the space and skills to develop leadership for the benefit of entire communities.

By purchasing this book, you contribute towards developing the leadership of women and girls around the world to achieve human rights, health, security, dignity, freedom, justice and peace for **all** people.

Bonnie Lou Fatio